Basic aspects of psychoanalytic group therapy

The International Library of Group Psychotherapy and Group Process

General Editors

Dr Malcolm Pines
The Tavistock Clinic, London

Dr Earl Hopper
The London School of Economics and Political Science

The International Library of Group Psychotherapy and Group Process
is published in association with the Institute of Group Analysis
(London)

Basic aspects of psychoanalytic group therapy

Peter Kutter

Translated by Angela Molnos

Routledge & Kegan Paul
London, Boston, Melbourne and Henley

To my patients in Stuttgart

This translation first published in 1982
by Routledge & Kegan Paul Ltd
39 Store Street, London, WC1E 7DD,
9 Park Street, Boston, Mass. 02108, USA,
296 Beaconsfield Parade, Middle Park,
Melbourne, 3206, Australia and
Broadway House, Newtown Road
Henley-on-Thames, Oxon RG9 1EN
Set in Press Roman 10/12 by
Columns, Reading
and printed in Great Britain by
T.J. Press (Padstow) Ltd
Padstow, Cornwall
First published as Elemente der Gruppentherapie
Translated from the German with permission
of Vandenhoeck & Ruprecht Verlag, Göttingen
© Vandenhoeck & Ruprecht in Göttingen 1976
English translation © Routledge & Kegan Paul 1982

Library of Congress Cataloging in Publication Data

Kutter, Peter.

Basic aspects of psychoanalytic group therapy.
(The International library of group psycho-
therapy and group process)
Translation of: Elemente der Gruppentherapie.
Includes bibliographical references and index.
1. Group psychotherapy. I. Title. II. Series.
RC488.K8713   616.89'152   82-3672

ISBN 0-7100-9244-X   AACR2

Contents

Preface to the English edition

Nowadays it happens far more often that a work originally published in English is translated into German than vice versa. In the latter event there are always particular reasons which need mentioning. One justification for bringing this book to the English-speaking reader is that the international literature on psychoanalytically orientated group psychotherapy tends to be theoretical and presents a contradictory picture in itself. In contrast − as a German reviewer put it (Gerd Heising, *Psyche*, vol. 33, 1979, p. 671) − this book gives a non-dogmatic and practical outline, attempts to bring together psychoanalytic concepts which so far have remained unrelated and offers a clear illustration of the theory through case material. It was presumably for these same reasons that some members of the London-based Group-analytic Society − namely Johanna Brieger, Lisbeth Hearst, Adele Mittwoch and Gregory van der Kleij − took an interest in this work and put forward the idea that it should also appear in English. It was to Johanna Brieger's credit that she pursued this suggestion further.

Fortunately a very special translator was found in the person of Angela Molnos who is as well versed in both languages, and the art of translating, as she is competent in the subject matter. She succeeded brilliantly in expressing in English what the author intended to say in German. Malcolm Pines too lent her his invaluable support. Co-operation between translator and author left nothing to be desired. As a result, this English version is an outstanding example of a vivid transposition from one language to another. Some passages describing group events and individual histories come out even more directly and forcefully than they did in the original text. The clinical aspects of the three group processes appear with even greater sharpness.

Theory remains in the background and serves only to throw light on problems which are relevant to the practice, such as working through the early mother-child relationship and the Oedipus complex in the group situation, the theory of the group process, the various forms of transference, including the group conductor's counter-transference. I trust, therefore, that this work will find an equally positive and friendly reception in the wider English-speaking world as it has done among German-speaking readers. I hope it will be found useful by all those who have to do with group psychotherapy as conductors or members of groups as well as those who are simply interested in this field.

Peter Kutter
Frankfurt, 1980

Preface to the German edition

In the literature on psychoanalytic group therapy there are surprisingly few contributions from actual practice. Up to now even my own publications have been mainly theoretical.[1] Therefore, it seems to me that it is high time to look at 'practice'. This is the intention of the present book. The volume is based on more than five years of experience with therapy groups in my private practice, and more precisely, on three groups of mixed-sex composition. These groups, meeting once and twice weekly, lasted from two to four years.

Winfried Hellmann, who had read the original manuscript with the eyes of a professional reader and publisher, encouraged me to revise it for a broader audience. The aims of the revision were: to introduce the reader to psychoanalytic group therapy without assuming too much previous knowledge or information; to present the subject in a progressive and illustrative way; and, to give a central place to case material that is rarely otherwise published. Theory is included only to the extent to which it was considered useful in understanding concrete examples. The material is organized in such a way that the various aspects of group therapy, so to speak its building stones, become visible one after the other through the chapters.

I am aware of the prejudice still prevailing according to which it is unscientific to renounce technical language. Despite this, I tried my best to write in generally comprehensible language. Technical terms which could not be avoided are explained. Nevertheless, I hope that the presentation will be of interest to colleagues, especially as a comparison with their own experiences. Furthermore, it might offer a glimpse into practice to those group analysts who are still in training. Last but not least, it is written for those who are interested in psychoanalytic group therapy and would like to understand what it is all about. I believe that to obtain information on its practice, rather than on its theory, is a good way to learn the basics of psychoanalytic group therapy. The reader will get a vivid picture of how the 'business of psycho-analytic group therapy' is managed and also have an opportunity to put himself in the situation of the group conductor, thus learning by imitation or identification.

In order to give a clear overall view of the vast field of psycho-analytic group therapy, and to make group therapy intelligible as a specific psychoanalytic method, I started from definite basic aspects. Then, for the presentation, I evaluated the material of the three above-mentioned groups. Typical scenes, episodes and situations were selected in relation to the various aspects under discussion. Because of this method of presentation, it was unavoidable that the continuity of the group process became less prominent than the basic aspects described. Nevertheless, I hope that the sum total of these aspects will give the reader a comprehensive picture of what psychoanalytic group therapy is and how it works.

Chapter 1

Indication for treatment
and the contract

The complex process that takes place within psychoanalytic group therapy runs through an initial phase, a middle or main phase, and an end phase. The process begins with the composition of the group which is either predetermined by the conductor who selects the group members, or by a colleague of his who puts a group together for him. In all cases the structure of a group is given from the start through its members.

Here we have to consider the selection of patients together with the question of indications for psychoanalytic group therapy. Both, indication and selection, are of great significance for the fate of the group and its entire development.

As in individual therapy, the candidate for group therapy should be able to establish a working alliance[1] with the analyst. The patient should have a sufficiently strong motivation to participate in psychoanalytic group therapy. Such a motivation implies that he sees this method as a way of overcoming his difficulties. Moreover, the patient should be able to imagine himself in the group situation. There he is, together with six to ten other people and will have to talk not only about his symptoms, but also about his emotional problems, without too much verbal inhibition and without being too ashamed.

The analyst and the patients agree on a contract that includes the following points: each patient is prepared to settle down in the group to the best of his ability; to attend the sessions regularly; to arrive on time; and, in the interest of the common good, to feel responsible *vis-à-vis* the conductor and the other members. The criteria for individual therapy should be added here, namely: motivation of the patient heightened through the pressure of suffering; interest in discovering the psychological background of one's complaints; a certain capacity for insight in relation to oneself and others; as well as perseverance and purposefulness. Each group member has to be ready to participate in the group process. As this process affects the whole person, members

1

should be aware of the fact that temporary worsening of symptoms can occur and that this process can trigger off fundamental changes in their existing human relations outside the group.

Further preconditions are: a certain degree of ego-strength, which enables one to control and direct one's instinctual impulses, to cope with emotional stress and to defer gratification of drives of hatred and love as well as to channel them towards the attainment of socially more elevated goals. Klaus Frank mentions another criterion[2] : the patient has to be able to move and change back and forth between himself and the structure of the group-as-a-whole. In other words, he should be able constructively to perceive and manage himself in the group, as well as the group-as-a-whole. According to this criterion, personalities with a weak ego, with a propensity to impulsive explosions, and with little capacity to cope with frustration — that is to say to tolerate their own failures — would not be suitable for psychoanalytic group therapy. Such members might damage the group through the destructive aggressiveness which is peculiar to them. Should they be admitted to group therapy, sooner or later the group itself will push them out for the sake of its survival. On the other hand, a destructively aggressive member is not always forced to leave the group. Quite often the contrary happens. The group singles out such a member — predestined for its purpose — in order to project on to him, or her, unconscious parts of the other participants' personalities. These projected aspects of personality are those against which group members defend themselves. The projection allows group members to fight against the rejected parts of themselves in the other person. This is the well-known defence mechanism of finding a scape-goat. This mechanism has to be worked through by the group, lest injustice befall the member singled out by the group.

The contract between patients and analyst also includes the so-called fundamental rule. As in individual therapy, this rule has to be honoured in order for the process to start. The fundamental rule, applied to the group, runs as follows: Each group member says as freely and spontaneously as possible whatever occurs to him, regardless of whether it is pleasant or not, whether it belongs to the dominant theme of the moment, whether it is embarrassing or whether it appears somehow irrelevant. In other words, group members agree that as far as possible they will lift the control exerted by critical thinking. Instead of 'free associations'[3] , in psychoanalytic group therapy we speak of 'group associations' or 'free-floating discussion'. This type of discussion can be considered as the equivalent of the Freudian 'free associations' in individual analysis.[4] The interactions, underlying the free-floating discussion, are always determined through the presence of others. To put it differently, the individual member is free only to the extent to which the others allow him to be. On the other hand, despite the presence of others, each member is free to talk, but by doing so he limits the others. The alternating talking and not-talking of one group member and the others is characteristic of free discussion in a group.

Chapter 2

Understanding, observing, interpreting

In order to be able to grasp the great variety of phenomena which occur in groups and to find one's way among them, a general frame of reference is needed. Basically, there are three major paths which, in my opinion, complement each other and together constitute such a framework: understanding, observing, and interpreting.

1 The path of understanding

The first path for the conductor is that of understanding the group members through psychoanalytic empathy which is also called the hermeneutic method. As a conductor I try to understand what the group members feel and where they stand. I do this through empathy, by putting myself in their place so that I may feel as they do. I also try to understand what the other person says, what his talk manifestly means and what is the concealed meaning behind it. Since Freud, we know that we do not understand our patients if we only note the literal meaning of their statements. We will only understand them if we try to find out what meaning lies beyond their statements. The concealed meaning of what they say remains a mystery to them because they could not cope with it emotionally. This meaning is mostly aggravating and hurtful, so the real content is disguised in the same way as the dream disguises its true meaning behind images. The meaning of a dream image has to be uncovered progressively through interpretation. As far as possible, the concealed meaning should be interpreted with the co-operation of the patient. The latter has to bring his free associations and his ideas to the interpretation.

As a conductor I also try to understand individual members of the group and to find out what makes them tick. As for the group as a whole, I start with the theoretical assumption that the discussion in the group revolves at all times around a common theme of which the group members are not conscious. We talk of 'common group tension', of a 'common denominator'[1] or of a 'common unconscious fantasy'[2] in which all group members have a share, but to which each of them as an individual reacts differently.

Through empathy the conductor should be able to understand both the common unconscious fantasy as well as the specific individual reaction of each participant to it. As a result of the repetition compulsion,[3] experiences which were too rejecting or too pampering to be worked through in childhood continue to affect the person's current behaviour. Therefore, we can start by assuming that each participant unconsciously attempts to act out those scenes to which he is traumatically fixated. Understanding the 'scene'[4] means that as a conductor I try to understand the situation which is developing by letting myself be part of it to a certain extent. At the same time, relying on my knowledge of the crucial stages of psychic development and social relationships, I try to find out which one of these developmental stages is being re-enacted. If I manage to do both, then I succeed in being as close as I possibly can to the participant's actual experience. The knowledge of how drives, love, hatred, the personality itself and interpersonal relationships develop is particularly helpful. Interpersonal relationships and their development are particularly important, such as: two-person relationships between mother and child, between child and father, as well as triangular relationships between mother, father and child, and, finally, multiple relationships within the family as a whole – especially with and among siblings – and the relationships in other groups, such as in the kindergarten, at school and so on.

Based on several years of self-training in this kind of observation, I try to pick out the pattern of relationships prevalent in the group at a given moment. Then I see whether my empathic feeling can be brought into harmony with my knowledge of the psychology of drives, ego-psychology and the psychology of object relations. After having examined it in the light of theory, I try to interpret my perception to the group. I try to say in appropriate sentences what I have perceived in an empathic and psychoanalytic way. In all this process it is my own feelings first and foremost which help me to understand what feelings prevail in the group.

2 The path of observing

The conductor not only feels the scene in an empathic way, but he is also an observer. He observes the group members' behaviour, their facial expressions, gestures, postures, and speech: whether they sit in a tense, stiff manner or are relaxed and at ease; whether they speak in a low or loud voice, one at a time or all together in a confusion. He pays attention to signs of excitement or anxiety, such as blushing, flushing, trembling hands, sweating. In the first place, the conductor listens to the contents of the speech, to sentence and word and to how they are cathected by emotions. He is on the look out for the emotions underlying the contents. Jealousy and envy, hatred and love, revenge and attempts at reparation play a central part. The conductor should always be aware of defences being directed against the core of the communication which, therefore, is not expressed directly. Nevertheless, when former relationships with parents and siblings, aunts, uncles and grandparents are re-lived in the relationship with the conductor and other group members, the original emotions, anxieties or desires often become apparent in the excitement of the here and now.

3 The path of interpreting

The analyst's specialized knowledge of developmental and social psychology allows him to make interpretations. He has knowledge of the psychic mechanisms as described by psychoanalysis, and more precisely by the instinct-psychology, ego-psychology and the psychology of object relations. The knowledge of the so-called psycho-sexual development stages, as described by Sigmund Freud in his *Three Essays on the Theory of Sexuality*[5] is essential. The significance of the 'oral' stage is not only food intake and gratification through the mouth, but also the question of whether one is accepted or rejected. The 'anal' stage does not hinge only on the excretory functions, but it has to do with self-assertion, with carrying through one's purpose, dominating or being dominated, with destroying or being destroyed. Finally, in the 'genital' stage the specificity of the sexes develops. The male-female polarity determines the instinctual life of the child during this stage. After a latency period, these three development stages are relived in an intensified form during puberty. Their reappearance has to do with a suddenly heightened drive progression resulting from physiological changes. Then, during adolescence and early adulthood, the three stages are integrated progessively into the personality.

Following Erik Erikson,[6] one can conceive of the Freudian development stages as being a series of eight psycho-social crises through which a healthy personality grows. Each of these crises takes place between two opposite poles. The first of these opposites is trust versus basic mistrust, followed by autonomy versus shame and doubt, initiative versus guilt, industry versus inferiority, identity versus role diffusion, intimacy versus isolation, generativity versus stagnation, and the final stage of ego integrity versus despair. As Erikson's categories − unlike the Freudian development stages − make the social aspect of development very clear, they are most suitable to be applied to psychoanalytic group therapy.

Erikson's categories are particularly helpful to sort out group processes.[7] After all the group is a social field in which crises and personality growth takes place. The problem of trust plays an important role right from a group's inception. Equally important is the question of the individual's identity in the group and the group's identity as a whole. The polarity intimacy versus isolation is one of the central themes concerning the individual in the group. Remarkably enough, it is by no means only the later stages of childhood and their multiple relationships which are revealed. Even the earliest relationship with the mother[8] as well as the relationship with the father,[9] comes to the surface in the group.

As a conductor I observe not only the relationship patterns as they are reactivated, but also their cathexis: whether they are characterized by love or hate; whether they are ruled by jealousy, and so on. For instance, jealousy in the group can be that of the child whose mother turns away from it in order to turn her attention to father. Often the envy that originally was directed against the mother is transferred to the analyst: he is envied for his skills, professional position, his wealth of experience and his relative independence. We shall return to this point in greater detail later on.

Chapter 3
Three theoretical models of psychoanalytic group therapy

1 Therapy of the individual in the group

The understanding, observing and interpreting of the group process goes hand-in-hand with the understanding, observing and interpreting of the changes that occur in each individual member. This view does not imply that I use the group only to treat a single individual at a time, as if the other members were not there or as if they assumed only psycho-analytic functions together with the conductor. Admittedly, this is one of the possible ways of sorting out the multiple processes in the group. This is the way, for instance, Alexander Wolf and Emanuel Schwartz work.[1] On the other hand, I have to mark off my position also *vis-à-vis* those writers who see the group only as a whole and consider the individual at most as the 'speaker' of the group.[2] In my view, the con-ductor has to pay the same attention to the individual as to the group. For this reason I prefer to see each participant in an individual inter-view before he joins the group. Such a pre-group interview gives each member an opportunity to establish a working alliance as well as a personal rapport with me. It also enables the participant to transfer on to me as an individual feelings which originally were directed to a significant object in his or her past. This is the only way I can deal with patients in a private consulting practice. After all, each patient seeks me in order to get help from me as a doctor and a psychoanalyst or, more accurately, in order to learn to understand himself or herself better with my help. I would fail to respond to these legitimate expectations if I considered the patient only as a group member.

2 Therapy of the group through the group with the individual's participation

From the very beginning the group develops its own dynamics. To differentiate it from the psycho-dynamics of the individual, we call it group dynamics. This dynamics appears within the group and each individual participates in it whether he or she chooses to do so or not. Communications theory teaches us that human beings cannot not communicate. They have no choice but to communicate.[3] As Aristotle says, man is a *zoon politikon*, a creature that lives in community together with others.

According to system theory, a group is a product resulting from the dynamic interactions of its parts and is a system in itself. It is therefore not just the sum of its parts. Group dynamics consists of a continuous interchange, a to and fro of processes such as giving and taking, oppressing and being oppressed, loving and being loved, leaving and being left, eliminating and being eliminated. All these processes affect each other. In this system I can never learn to know simultaneously a part's impulse as well as its place. This is the uncertainty principle one of the early quantum theorists, Werner Heisenberg,[4] established in matrix mechanics and it applies also to the group. I hear a participant's talk and, at the same time, I have to take into account the place from which he speaks. This 'place' from which the individual speaks is determined by the group or, to be more exact, by the group's unconscious fantasy. If I pay attention to this fantasy, then I cannot concentrate simultaneously and equally well on the individuals' reactions to the same fantasy. Yet it is my task to link both. If I completely overlooked the individual in favour of the group, I would do violence to the former. By ignoring the individual in the group, I would expose him to the perils of levelling away individual differences in favour of uniformity. Such a procedure would be an affront to the uniqueness of the individual. For this reason, I do not share the group's enthusiastic glorification which at times is truly exaggerated at least in some countries. Those who one-sidedly exalt the group see all the good in collectivism and nothing in the individual. Much as I appreciate the importance of a group's influence on the individual and much as I acknowledge the group's capacity to see more than the individual does, I shall be on guard against overrating the group at the expense of the individual. The latter course is a real danger to which we are very much exposed. In fact, it is a far more exacting task to have to observe not only the group process but, in addition, to consider also the specific psychic situation of each of the six to ten individuals. This task requires a multi-track thinking and feeling which puts an almost excessive demand on a single conductor. In order to circumvent this difficulty, many group researchers[5] changed the complicated multi-purpose relationship into a two-person relationship, namely by regarding the group as an individual who sits opposite the conductor. The other extreme, that is to see only the parts and not the whole, would be equally wrong. One would commit the same mistake for which Mephisto mocks the student in Goethe's *Faust*:[6]

> To docket living things past any doubt
> You cancel first the living spirit out:
> The parts lie in the hollow of your hand,
> You only lack the living link you banned.

3 The two-dimensional model of psychoanalytic group therapy

The group conductor cannot shun the double task of having to see both, the individual as well as the group, each in its own right as a whole. Hence he will end up with a blend of model 1 (therapy of the individual in the group) and model 2 (therapy of the group through the group with the individual's participation). In this way we obtain a model 3 which links both approaches. This model is advocated by S.H. Foulkes,[7] a psycho-analyst born in Karlsruhe, Germany, in 1898. In 1933 he emigrated to London where he died in 1976. Each participant brings a network of relationships into the group. This together with the relationships of the other members forms a total 'network'. This network characteristic of the group as a whole is the basis on which new relationships are established. It is like a matrix on which the mesh of new relationships is secured. It is from this perspective that I see the individual and the point of the network where he is. At the same time I also try to see the network itself, that is to say, the mesh of relationships that stretches between the individual participants.

Bearing this theoretical model in mind, let us now attempt to approach the practice. Our purpose should be to link theory with practice. To start with let us put ourselves in the situation of people who decide to accept psychoanalytic group therapy. To understand this situation we will look at the first session of a group. The first session is in fact the best starting point. From there on — after having gone through an unavoidable piece of grey theory — I hope to be able to offer the reader a lively and direct insight into the events of a group. At the same time this is an opportunity for me to introduce to the reader the first of three groups.

Chapter 4

The first session of Group 1

1 Sequence of events

Each member brings his individual history and unresolved conflicts into the group as well as his anxieties and hopes. Who will be there? What will happen to me? How am I going to assert myself? It is only natural that to a certain extent every participant is anxious before the first session. The group conductor too has his anxieties and expectations. Of course, he has the advantage of already knowing the participants. He also has theoretical knowledge at his disposal to help him. Moreover, as a participant observer he can keep himself relatively detached from the process in which the group members inevitably get involved. Thanks to his detachment he is able to take an overall view of the situation.

The fact that the process of analytic group therapy is unstructured — i.e. the group is conducted without predetermined framework to which members could get used — leads inevitably to anxiety. The participants defend themselves against this anxiety by regressing, that is to say they relapse into an earlier stage of their psychic development. This is a desirable therapeutic effect because it is only through regression that the unresolved conflicts can come to life again.

Already at the start of the very first session regression might appear leading back to the earliest stage of the child's development. The group is likely to counteract such a massive form of regression through a first joint defence process in which all participants engage and which could be called 'group-defence'. The defence could start by first reaching the level which is least anxiety-evoking for everyone. On this level the group can deal for instance with more superficial problems, such as the complaints of some participants. Already in the first session, each participant's characteristic behaviour begins to take shape. This initial behaviour foreshadows the structure which will become progressively clearer in the course of the group process. Such a structure is specific

12

to each group.[1] To illustrate this initial behaviour the first session of
Group 1 will now be outlined. I conducted this group, composed of
four women and four men, from June 1969 till June 1972 over 205
sessions of 100 minutes each. Group 1 was characterized by a marked
contrast between men and women. This dichotomy was reflected already in the first session of the group — not only in the contents of
the discussion, but also in the participants' behaviour.

All the patients are gathered in the consulting room before the
session starts. I enter the room at the agreed time and sit on the chair
which is left free. After my entry there is an uneasy silence. All glances
are directed towards me. There is insecurity written on every face.
Every glance indicates expectation. All keep silent. During this silence
I observe the sitting order of the group.[2] Opposite to me is Mr Gage,
25, structural engineer, sitting in a rigid posture, his head flushed, near
tears. To my left is Mrs Faulkner, 40. She has stopped studying
psychology and is now a journalist. She is pale with long, blonde hair,
smartly dressed. The chairs, all identical, have been arranged in a circle
before the patients' arrival. Next to Mrs Faulkner is Mr Pittman, 35,
businessman, slim, well-groomed, visibly tense. Near Mr Gage and
opposite to me, is Mrs Sheen, 25, a factory-girl. She is very nice to look
at and attractively dressed. To her left there is a middle-aged woman.
She dropped out from the group after a short time and was replaced
which is why I disregard her now. To my right there is Mrs Murphy.
She is a 31-year-old, sophisticated woman. She has become a computer
programmer after having given up her studies in education. Next to her
there is Mr Morgan, a 34-year-old manager as well-groomed as Mr
Pittman. He is looking at me in a particularly quizzical manner. A
bearded young man, seated between Mr Morgan and Mrs Sheen, com-
pletes the circle. As he failed to return after this first session, we need
not concern ourselves with him.

In this first session the principal actors turn out to be the 25-year-
old factory-girl, the 40-year-old journalist, the young Mr Gage and the
34-year-old manager, Mr Morgan. The following discussion took place
among them which I reconstruct from memory and with the aid of the
written record which was prepared after each session.

Mrs Faulkner asks whether she may smoke a cigarette. The others
reply in a completely conventional fashion with a nod and a 'Yes, do'.
Thereupon Mrs Murphy also lights a cigarette. The others do not
smoke. Thus, smokers and non-smokers emerge as the first pair of
opposites in the first session of this group. There is a sub-group of two
women who smoke and the rest, the non-smoking sub-group which

tolerates the former's action. Now the pretty factory-girl starts to talk about her marriage problems. She complains about her husband who is too indolent to pay any attention to her. His attitude is more than irritating; in fact, it makes her livid with rage. She certainly cannot bring herself to be nice to him. On the contrary, she is cold and rejecting towards him. We hear from Mrs Sheen how often her husband is away. He comes home late at night. It is apparent that he fancies other women and has no regard whatsoever for his wife's feelings. Mrs Faulkner takes sides with her and, in her turn, complains about her boyfriend. He is ten years her senior, lazy and tends to rely on her instead of supporting her. Thereupon, the exquisite Mrs Murphy starts to speak. Up to now leaning back in her seat, she was only smoking. She talks about frequently moving house and about her unrelatedness to other people. In my perception, while telling us something about herself she is also unconsciously hinting at the here and now situation of the group. I pick up this hint and transform it into the following interpretation which I share with the group: the situation is characterized by the fact that no one knows the others. Therefore, there is anxiety, all the more so as I was saying nothing. However, I think that what Mrs Murphy just told us about her unrelatedness to others, also has a bearing here in the group. At this point, Mrs Faulkner, the journalist and former psychology student, who sits at my left, points out that so far the male participants of the group have not said anything at all. After an uneasy silence the young engineer talks about the great problem he has with girls. He just does not know how to approach them. He also mentions his professional difficulties, his inability to achieve anything. Then he talks about his sufferings: tension headaches, disturbed concentration . . . his voice deadens. He only just manages to suppress crying. Mr Morgan notices it and as though continuing Mr Gage's unfinished speech, tells the group about his disturbed potency, his difficulties with his wife who no longer holds any feminine attraction for him. Thereupon Mr Gage is able to talk again and to express his great doubts about group therapy. Although he decided to commit himself to group therapy, he cannot imagine how such an approach could possibly help. This last part is directed towards me with an unequivocally reproachful overtone in his voice, accompanied by a strangely help-seeking glance. At this point I make the following comment: After having listened to all that has been said, it appears to me that the men have no less difficulties with their women than the women have with their men. Thereupon Mr Gage is able to say that he feels he is being put under pressure here. He does not spell out where the pressure comes from. His statement is followed again by a prolonged silence which is interrupted by the factory-girl. She knows all this from her quarrels with men. After her first marriage broke up, she had a boy-friend for a long time. All that this man did was to satisfy his own sexual needs, thus taking advantage of her. At first it looked as if the third man, to whom she is now married, would bring her the love she longed for. Gradually it became clear, however, that he was not capable of appreciating her either. He too used her only for his own sexual pleasure, letting her down afterwards. During this speech she gets into a state of mounting rage against her husband. She admits that she dislikes herself being in this state. Yet, it is not her fault that she feels nothing but disgust and repulsion while having intercourse with her husband. Mr Pittman, who kept silent up to now, ends this first group session by talking about his professional anxieties. He is afraid of losing his job. Unlike his colleagues, he has no diploma in business administration and yet, he would like to be promoted to a higher managerial position. After her statement about being unable to relate to people, Mrs Murphy, smoking one cigarette after the other, has been sitting silently in the circle, as though taking shelter in her chair. She followed the events, however, with marked interest. I closed the session with the following comments: Everyone has difficulties with other people. Obviously these difficulties lead to mutual disappointments for which each resents the other. Considering the doubts Mr Gage had already expressed, I would not be surprised if psycho-analytic group therapy would also disappoint the participants' expectations. By talking about our problems openly, we do have, however, a chance to bring them to a solution. In fact, we have already made a hopeful start. Thereafter, one by one the participants leave the room while saying good-bye to me. Some go alone, others draw near to each other.

2 Theoretical considerations

If we take in at a glance the whole process in this first session, we will see a 'specific structure' already emerging 'as the result of the individual personalities participating in it'.[3] All of them experience anxiety in the face of the unknown. Everyone is afraid of a) the new situation; b) me as a conductor – whom he does not know and from whom he expects a lot; c) and the others – who are equally unknown to him. The session starts with someone wanting to smoke. This wish is perceived by the psychoanalytically orientated conductor as the 'oral' theme. The desire to smoke expresses the need to receive something from the conductor. As he keeps silent, i.e. does not give anything, one participant resorts to a cigarette as a substitute. I did not comment on this conflict because it appeared to be still far too removed from the feelings the group was able to experience on a conscious level. The second theme is the women's dissatisfaction with their men. The latter are seen as only being in the pursuit of their own needs. As they themselves are weak and look for someone to lean on, they are unable to offer the support the women would need. The women are disillusioned, enraged and withdrawn. This reaction is most pronounced in the case of Mrs Sheen, the pretty factory-girl. Mr Gage who is rough-mannered, yet very sensitive and easily moved to tears, resonates to the reproaches against men. He feels oppressed and greatly threatened by these reproaches. Quite obviously he expects help from me. This expectation manifests itself through his reproachful tone and his help-seeking glance. There is a conflict in which one side oppresses the other, without being yet clear whether the women oppress the men or vice versa. Unconsciously the participants are preoccupied with the question of with whom shall I side. In such a situation it is quite impossible to prevent the participants' sexual problems – potency disorders of the men and frigidity up to open rejection of sex among the women – combining to exacerbate the strife for supremacy between man and woman. In the subsequent course of the group process, this fight reached extraordinary proportions. Some sessions reminded me of the hatred between the sexes in Strindberg and in no way fell short of his scenes.

In my opinion, Mrs Murphy's contribution, stating her unrelatedness, was the most significant one. It reflected very well the general feeling in the room. At the same time it expressed the idea that men and women do not understand each other and neither do men or women among themselves. Finally, this contribution also implied that the relationship between the group and myself has not yet been established. This great doubt about the relationship with me arose from mistrust and anxiety as well as from exaggerated expectations. From a psychoanalytic point of view I see in this doubt the repetition of past disappointments and a first 'common denominator'[4] within the group. In the next chapter we will discuss the continuation of this process.

Chapter 5
Hatred and love between the sexes: continuation of the process in Group 1

1 Hatred of the strict and rejecting mother

Having presented the first session in detail, I will now try to outline broadly the further group process so that the reader may recognize the main themes that thread their way through it.

The women kept moving along the same line of hatred against the men. In the fourth session, Mrs Murphy, the ex-student of education, who most of the time had sat in silence, styled this hatred 'holy rage'. Its cause is the men's weakness. This weakness is best illustrated with the example of Mrs Faulkner's impotent boy-friend, a war invalid, but it also shows in the men's actual behaviour in the group. While cautiously biding their time, they seek help from me, the conductor. The men do this in a soft, unmanly fashion. After the tenth session the tide turns temporarily. Now the men seem to have recovered and in their turn they attack the women, forming a united front against the latter. Mr Morgan tucks up his shirtsleeves and sides with the women's oppressed and devalued men. He defends the much abused second husband of our pretty factory-girl; the devalued boy-friend of the journalist, Mrs Faulkner; and, later on, Mrs Murphy's boy-friend. After the twenty-second session the women's party is strengthened by Mrs Sinfield, 33-year-old housewife, replacing the female participant who had dropped out. Despite her severe depressions and cardiac anxiety, Mrs Sinfield fitted in well with the women's militant behaviour. All the more so as her depressions concealed a barely contained rage against her husband. In her unconscious fantasy he represented her father. The men were still holding their offensive against the women, thus causing anxiety among the latter. Mrs Murphy dreamed of the fear of being murdered by a man; Mrs Sheen's headaches and giddiness grew more frequent; Mrs Faulkner became increasingly tense; and, due to the strained atmosphere, the newly arrived Mrs Sinfield had difficulties in settling

in. Around the fortieth session the women came out on top again. This
time it was the men's turn to feel anxious. Their state was revealed in
the cardiac anxiety Mr Pittman suffered for a while, Mr Morgan's intensified potency disturbances and the temporary, yet nearly total
inability to work of Mr Gage, the young structural engineer. Then
around the fiftieth session the unhappy situation of stalemate between
the sexes took a positive turn. Now both parties directed their aggression against the conductor. The attack was led by the dynamic Mr
Gage. He abused me as being someone who does not do anything, but
pocketing money, sitting and grinning like a stuffed dummy. At the
same time *he* works like a slave in his business without achieving anything, experiencing one disillusionment after another with girls and
being less and less able to think straight. It was Mr Gage who ventured
to speak openly about his feelings of being oppressed by me. I am the
one who dictates the time, who through silence taxes his patience, who
closes the sessions and who cancels sessions when it suits him without
taking any notice of the patients' needs. He now demands an explana-
tion of the whole procedure. Why have I composed the group as I did
and not in another way? Here he feels oppressed and without any hope
of being freed from his difficulties. The other men partly agree with
Mr Gage. Now they too feel oppressed by me and by Mrs Faulkner, the
journalist, who meanwhile has become a kind of 'co-therapist'. Unconsciously they experience themselves as children ruled over and
manipulated by a couple of parents who make them hop like puppets.
After I had interpreted this configuration to the group, Mr Gage recalls
that at one time he felt oppressed by his mother and his sisters in just
the same way as he feels oppressed here and now by me and by the
women, especially by Mrs Faulkner. Friends let him down at one time
just as the other men do now in the group. Thus, it becomes clear why Mr
Gage was so full of hatred. He had relived his childhood situation
directly through me, Mrs Faulkner and the other women. At that time
he was oppressed by mother and sisters. As he puts it, these women did
not allow him 'to make his way up'. His mates — in the group the male
members — left him to his own devices. On an even deeper unconscious
level I also stood for his father whom he had lost when he was one year
old and whom he had idealized and glorified in fantasy. On the other
hand, this father was not there when needed to protect him against the
repressive upbringing his mother and sisters inflicted upon him.

All the time different configurations kept on emerging. Each of
them reflected a participant's specific childhood situation in which he
had suffered so intensely as to be unable to overcome it. For Mrs Sheen

I represented not the oppressive mother, but the untrustworthy mother who let her struggle alone with men. Attracted by her sex appeal, these men seduced her early in life. Having misused her sexually, they ruthlessly deserted her. No sooner had the men in the group expressed any sexual desire, than they became in her eyes the same hustlers and woman-chasers. She saw them as having nothing else in mind but to touch the woman, catch hold of her breasts, go to bed with her, with not a trace of consideration for her feelings or for her longing for tenderness and support.

Later on in the process the other participants were also drawn into the heavy struggle with the strict mother who lacks generosity. They experienced her in the person of the conductor. Mrs Murphy dreamed of a dead mother whom she had nursed devotedly during an illness, but whom she did not love. This relationship epitomized the relationships of all the others with their mothers. Mrs Sinfield's case illustrated the theme of the 'rejecting mother' in its clearest form. After initial hesitation she began to work through her feelings of shame and guilt. Thereafter she was able to confess that, basically, she hated her two children and occasionally she even gave them a sound thrashing. In the sixty-eighth session Mrs Sheen was also able to talk openly about her hatred towards her child. The child, born from the relationship with the unloved husband, had not been wanted in the first place.

This phase of the group process dragged on for a long time. At the core of all my interpretations during this period was the remark: 'This is what a mother does to her child.' This interpretation was related: a) to the ways the participants experienced me as a conductor; b) to the manner in which they themselves handled their children; c) to the manner in which their mother handled them. This central theme was shared by nearly every participant, including the new member who joined in the fifth session replacing the young man with the beard who had dropped out. The newcomer is Mr Hardwick, 32, an engineer. Since his childhood he has stammered and currently was under stress at work. In addition he suffers from headaches, sleep disorder and anxiety.

Reproaches and protests rained down because of my stand-offish attitude. I was experienced as being callous, cold and rejecting. Participants had death-wishes towards me and, at the same time, they felt guilty because of these wishes. There was also fear that with the death of the conductor their last chance of getting any help would be forfeited. After the murderous attacks against my person there was considerable gain in insight. By recalling memories related to their mothers, participants began to see the psychodynamics of what was happening.

They had felt just as much threatened, oppressed and persecuted by their mothers as by me. Thereupon phases of great harmony followed. In the sixty-eighth session one wanted to be cuddled; desires for tenderness were expressed in the seventy-second session. The men, especially Mr Pittman and Mr Morgan, were now more able to experience these feelings, to share and to reciprocate them.

2 Eroticism between the sexes

The group felt safe and protected. Of course, this feeling could not last long as the jealousy of individual members promptly interfered with it. Mr Gage in particular could not stand the harmony between the elder participants and myself. He felt excluded and towards the end of each session regularly destroyed our union with sentences that sounded like hammer-strokes. His jealousy was well-founded in as much as between each of the women and myself a transference love had developed. This love became increasingly noticeable. Mrs Sinfield dreamed that she and I strolled hand in hand through a meadow full of flowers. Mrs Sheen flirted with me in the group even if somewhat guardedly. The smart Mrs Murphy, while sulking over the impossibility of satisfying her needs and nestling tightly in her chair, from time to time twinkled at me seductively with her eyes. Only Mrs Faulkner was unable to have erotic feelings towards me. Instead, she co-operated with me, thus showing that she could get along with me very well. She felt completely as a 'co-therapist'. Her former studies of psychology seemed to make this role easy for her working alongside a conductor with a medical background.

The eroticism which was first activated in relation to the conductor, began to spread to the participants' relationships among themselves. For instance, Mr Morgan made no secret of his love for the attractive Mrs Sinfield and was often courting her. Also Mr Pittman started to weave tender bonds of love with Mrs Murphy. Having happily joined him at first, during the later turn of events Mrs Murphy withdrew from this relationship. She then took up the old fighting position against men. Also the other love relationships between male and female participants foundered. One obvious reason for this failure was that the agreed abstinence among participants during psychoanalytic group therapy made sexual gratification impossible. The main reason was, however, that previous negative experiences in love relationships repeated themselves in the group. In fact, each member had had his share of failures with the opposite sex. Moreover, rather than being brought about by successive partners, these bad experiences were self-induced in a pathological repetition compulsion. Negative experiences in love relationships were due to the fixation of the libido to a disappointing mother relationship. This was the general theme of the group from the ninety-first session onwards. Both sexes' aggressive, rejecting and thoroughly disparaging behaviour towards each other turned out to be nothing but revenge against the mother of one's childhood. One had experienced her as frustrating, oppressive and far too powerful. She seemed to have everything and give nothing. She humiliated one, left one in the lurch and brought one to near starvation. Now the mother was beaten in the person of someone else who stood in for her. This substitute could be the marriage partner, the conductor of the group, or one's own child. Once more the dynamic Mr Gage, who had felt excluded during most of the erotic phase, was completely with the group. In fact he had the strongest revenge impulses towards his rejecting strict mother. Now he functioned as if he were the group's steam-engine. The group's offensive which he led against me, was marked by the anxieties in the rank and file of his followers. It felt as though I could in fact have been murdered. In that case the group would have been robbed of its conductor. This danger sparked off efforts by the group to protect the threatened conductor, whereupon Mr Gage felt betrayed. The treachery allowed him to turn his attacks against his disloyal 'friends'. The subsequently deepening regression showed that the murderous hatred was more than a response to disappointments suffered in the past. Above all it was a deep-seated, repressed envy that kept the hatred alive. Again our dynamic Mr Gage felt this envy with particular intensity. It was the envy of the have-nots against those who possessed wealth, of the employee against the fat boss, of the dependent, suffering patient against the psychoanalyst who, in the patient's perception, sits there like a stuffed dummy. One envies him, as at one time one used to envy mother, because of his unfair advantage.

Here I would like to pause from the description of the processes in Group 1 in order to discuss the question of resistance and transference. Both are basic aspects of psychoanalytic group therapy, and of psychoanalysis in general. After that I would like to introduce the reader to Group 2 and show how in the course of the group process it fought for the father. Later on we will have an opportunity to return to Group 1 in the chapters on group processes and on early mother-child relationship.

Chapter 6

Resistance and defence in psychoanalytic group therapy

1 Resistance arising from shame, guilt and anxiety

The psychoanalyst calls resistance all those forms of behaviour that prevent the person from becoming aware of the causative and precipitating conflicts responsible for his symptoms. The reason for this resistance is the sense of shame that wounds our pride, our self-esteem and our egotism. Everyone would like to appear in a favourable light in front of himself and others. One is ashamed when one has to admit hating one's own child and battering it. In Group 1 we have seen how Mrs Sheen and Mrs Sinfield were ashamed of their feelings and behaviour; Mr Gage is ashamed of his murderous attacks; Mr Morgan, Mr Pittman and Mr Hardwick are ashamed when sexual desires flare up not towards their wives, but towards the women in the group.

One is ashamed for having such impulses not only in front of others, but also *vis-à-vis* one's own conscience. Therefore, guilt feelings, together with a sense of shame, are the main causes of resistance against becoming conscious of repressed sexual or aggressive impulses. In addition, the individual's anxiety makes him resist the psychoanalytic work and his consequent exposure. If someone expresses undisguised cravings for the gratification of his sexual or aggressive drives, then he will experience fear of punishment. There is also fear of the real danger that perhaps the therapist might not be able or willing to put up with the attacks. At the worst, the analyst might consider the patient 'not analysable'. In this case, even if he does not throw the patient out straightaway, he might suggest that the treatment be discontinued. In other cases the analyst might refuse to accept the patient at the outset. Most often the resistance stems from the anxiety caused by one's own instinctual impulses. These drives could break through so that one would lose control over them. They can be destructive forces, as in the case of Mr Gage, or sexual forces, as in the case of Mr Morgan *vis-à-vis* Mrs Sinfield.

Arising from shame and/or guilt feelings, fear of punishment or fear of instinctual break-through, there is resistance against uncovering these instinctual impulses. This resistance in its turn leads to a defence against those feelings, which assumes forms characteristic of each individual, depending on his innate predisposition and the education society imparted to him. The psychoanalyst speaks of mechanisms of defence and distinguishes roughly two categories:

(i) One category of defence mechanism is found in the classical neuroses such as hysteria, phobias and obsessional neuroses. Repression is the mechanism of defence prevalent in hysteria. The result is a physical symptom which links together the repressed instinctual impulses, the anxiety and the defence against it. In the case of the phobias there is a displacement from the anxiety-laden original childhood scene to another object, person or place. In obsessional neurosis, the child's forbidden instinctual impulses are regressed from the genital to the anal stage of psycho-sexual development. This regression leads to a split of affect and ideas as well as to a reversal in the direction of the impulses. In certain cases the displacement of forbidden instinctual impulses can be far reaching and include the need for punishment. Such displacements often appear in commonplace everyday transactions such as obsessional hand washing. In each case the final result of the defence is that the original impulses, which keep on seeking gratification, are banished from consciousness.

(ii) Another category of mechanisms of defence, which has been investigated only recently,[1] belongs to three 'post-classical forms of neuroses':[2] one form of post-classical neurosis arises from a faulty sense of identity in a 'fatherless society' and is characterized by defective identity or by identity disorder; another form of 'narcissistic' or 'symbiotic' neurosis is characterized by the fact that the early symbiotic union between mother and child remains undissolved well into adulthood; a third form of post-classical neurosis is characterized by deprivation from mothering in a 'motherless society'. These are the cases in which maternal love and care was deficient in early childhood. This deficiency leads to a faulty personality structure which can manifest itself in insecure identity, numerous behavioural disorders and in psychosomatic symptoms.

2 Resistance and repetition compulsion

The neurotic disorders displayed by members of Group 1 can be placed mostly in the category of the classical neuroses. Of course, these neuroses do not appear in pure form. Each group member presents a mixed form of neurosis in which hysterical, phobic and obsessional elements are combined. Moreover, Mr Gage also shows symptoms of post-classical neuroses. The symptoms of Mrs Sinfield (depressions, anxieties and heart complaints), Mrs Sheen (anxiety, trembling, slight irritability, headaches with muscle tension in the neck and shoulders), Mr Pittman (giddiness, fear of heart attack), Mr Hardwick (stammering, compulsive tidiness, fear of darkness), Mr Morgan (stomach and heart complaints, difficulties at work, impotence) can be classified as the classical symptomatic neuroses of hysteria (Mrs Sheen, Mrs Sinfield, Mr Morgan), phobia (Mr Pittman) and obsessional neurosis (Mr Hardwick).

The symptoms of the other three group members belong to the category of post-classical neuroses. Mrs Faulkner tends to take every possible heavy burden upon herself and to help others at her own expense. While doing so she painfully and masochistically enjoys her own sufferings. We speak of a so-called 'masochistic' character neurosis. Mrs Murphy lives in an unrelated fashion within her environment. She lives alone, centred around herself, but otherwise well adapted. She is, however, unable to become dependent on others. This behaviour is characteristic of the so-called 'narcissistic personality disorder' — a personality whose self-love is nurtured at the cost of a love for others.

Mr Gage is undoubtedly the most disturbed patient in this group. His identity is still far from being established. In other words, he suffers from an identity deficiency due to his fatherless childhood and to the lack of maternal care. Therefore, his case belongs to the second and third form of the post-classical neuroses. Moreover, his inability to establish permanent relationships, his drive eruptions, which are difficult to control, but above all his destructive rage, fed by an intensive envy which consumes him, support the diagnosis of a 'borderline' case. Such cases stand at the dividing line between neurosis and psychosis. They are characterized by the tendency to split feelings of hatred and love from each other, to deny having these feelings and to displace them on to other people. These people are then drawn into the 'borderline' person's destructive rage and made to be the instruments of his own murderous impulses.

Mr Gage experiences the others either as completely good or as completely bad. At times he feels persecuted by the latter. This feeling became even more pronounced in the course of later group processes indicating that he had to be considered 'severely disturbed'. The other participants, including Mrs Faulkner and Mrs Murphy, were also to a certain extent impaired by their symptoms. They too had their share of some severe personality disorder of the post-classical neurosis type. Nevertheless, these participants were able to enter and maintain sufficiently satisfactory relationships with other people and to do constructive work. Only their enjoyment of life was substantially curtailed due to characteristic sexual conflicts and the physical suffering inflicted by their symptoms.

Resistance is directed not only against specific instinctual needs or impulses, but also against the return of painful childhood experiences, in particular if they were so traumatic as to produce a basic fault.[3] These experiences were very hurtful and the child's personality was not equipped to cope with them at the time when they occurred. The child could not work them through internally, especially without help from parents or siblings. On the other hand, due to a repetition compulsion — which is hard to break — the traumatic experience impels one to enter the same painful situation again and again. The person in question does everything possible to relive in the present the original event experienced in the past. Unconsciously he brings other people like chess pawns into exactly the same configuration in which he had his painful experiences as a child. The seemingly nonsensical result is that he is exposed to the same pain. This repetition in itself is horrible and painful. It puts, however, the therapist in a position to recognize and understand the patient's original trauma which has been repressed and defended against because of resistance. The therapist can then show the person what happens in the here and now. Originally, Freud[4] thought that the ultimate reason for this repetition compulsion was an inborn death instinct which established itself 'beyond the pleasure principle'. On this point I rather share E. Bibring's view.[5] I believe that by following the repetition compulsion, and thus re-experiencing the original traumatic situation, a person has the chance to take up again the trauma that could not be overcome in childhood and to work through it as an adult.

3 An example of group defence

The work on resistance takes up a great deal of the group's time. The individual participant's defence structures form together a shared defence structure that I have termed 'group defence'. In Group 1 — characteristically for the classical neuroses prevalent among participants — repressions with symptom formation such as headaches and heart complaints readily developed during the resistance phase. The defence mechanism of denial characterized a later phase in which the deeper layers of the early mother-child relationship were reactivated.

The ninety-fourth session of this group will now be described because it is especially suited to illustrate these processes. The two women sitting opposite me, Mrs Sinfield and Mrs Sheen, hold health insurance application forms. (In Germany patients suffering from all kinds of neuroses can get financial support through health insurance.) They behave in a rather helpless fashion asking me what they should do with the forms. I take up the question, give them the information, but then I ask in my turn whether they could not have done it without my help. Mrs Sinfield declares that she could not possibly do it on her own. It is always her husband who does it. For a time the participants' contributions revolve around the question to what extent one should carry through tasks oneself or let others do so. During this discussion Mr Gage becomes increasingly restless and his head flushes, but for the moment he says nothing. Now Mr Pittman, the quiet businessman, takes up the role of the helpful gentleman. He explains in detail to the women how the administrative process takes place. He does not notice that meanwhile Mr Gage is growing restless beside him. In contrast, Mr Morgan is well aware of Mr Gage's state and asks him: 'How are you? Have you returned to work?' Mr Gage replies: 'Oh, it is bad, worse than ever. I had borrowed money, I did some work for my cousin and now he does not want to pay me! It is simply terrible.' His voice is choking. At this point Mrs Faulkner, the journalist, joins in abruptly, totally disregarding the two men. With great self-confidence she declares that things are far better now for her, also in relation to her boy-friend. For the time being she has nothing to complain about. During this free-floating discussion the factory-girl, the engineer and the housewife remained silent. To judge from their expressions they must feel depressed. The others notice their mood and in the end they fall into silence as well. In the midst of this silence I say: 'Some of you feel that you are not yet ready to act independently, while others, like Mr Pittman, prove that they can manage without me. Apparently this problem is not easy to solve, otherwise the group would not continue in this depressing silence.' Now Mr Gage, far more calm than before, starts to report that last Sunday he had seen Mrs Sinfield and Mr Morgan together on an excursion. There she appeared completely different from how she is here in the group. She was not depressed, but relaxed, happy and cheerful. This communication provokes the following reactions. Mrs Sheen suddenly gets goose-flesh. Mrs Murphy trembles in every limb like a leaf. Mrs Faulkner is near fainting and Mrs Sinfield reports a heart attack. I say: 'Mr Gage's communication arouses all sorts of anxieties.' After a lengthy, uneasy silence, Mrs Sinfield speaks: Yes, she and Mr Morgan got on very well together as two good friends and nothing more. She knows, however, that her husband is jealous because of their friendship. It was also awkward for her when she suddenly saw Mr Gage. A bewildered silence follows. I interpret: It is now obvious that behind the question whether to do things by oneself or let others do them, quite different emotions were concealed. These emotions, affection and sexual desire, are felt as being embarrassing. It appears that we have a pair in our midst who met outside and who very much enjoyed each other's company. In relation to the group, however, they both feel ashamed and guilty. The others in their turn are jealous of them. Mrs Sinfield confirms that what I say is true. When she does something like that she is always anxious and tries to conceal it. She has got so used to her own pretence that she can hardly admit any longer that in fact she wants to be independent from her husband and would like to meet other men, like Mr Morgan.

Suddenly Mr Gage bursts headlong into this scene in which up to now sexual feelings were conceded only timidly: 'When *I* brought in my feelings, the group turned a deaf ear. My needs for love were always dismissed. That hurts very much!' Mrs Faulkner retorts that by expressing his needs so clumsily, all that he does is to trigger off in the other person an outright defence reaction. He should not try to force a girl to love him. Mrs Sheen agrees: Mrs Faulkner is right. After rushing at a girl like that, Mr Gage needn't be surprised if she is no longer interested in him. On such occasions Mrs Sheen always feels herself an object, exploited for the satisfaction of the man's needs. She expects another kind of attitude which takes her own feelings into greater account. I offer a further interpretation and talk about the difficulties the group has in expressing any sexual needs at all. I link these difficulties with the dictates of an austere moral conscience. The group experiences this restrictive conscience in my person and in the person of Mr Pittman. This interpretation is meant to show the group members their conflict between instinctual impulses and the moral defence directed against them. Everyone now sees this conflict quite clearly except Mr Gage. Again he becomes increasingly restless, wriggles about in his chair and says loudly, almost yelling: 'I simply can't stand Mrs Faulkner looking at Dr Kutter all the time. I find this behaviour unbearable!' Mr Pittman, the quiet tradesman, does not let any of this upset him. He picks up the question of how men deal with women. He thinks one should be cautious when making contact. One should value the other person and take her feelings into account. Mrs Sheen remarks that that is exactly what her husband does not do. He only wants to have sexual intercourse with her and after he has had it, he coolly smokes a cigarette. She simply finds it revolting. Mrs Sinfield agrees. When it goes like that, she also feels that she is nothing but a commodity. But she takes exception to it. At this point I remark that what Mr Gage said about his relationship with women had just been acted out. Unconsciously he wanted to show the group how furious he was because he had been excluded by the Morgan-Sinfield couple. The same situation occurred again just now when he felt excluded in relation to Mrs Faulkner and myself. This interpretation puts the group visibly at its ease. The theme of how man and woman treat each other continues. Mrs Faulkner points out that she cannot understand why Mrs Sheen and Mrs Sinfield so vehemently oppose the man's sexual desire. Both women retort that they cannot understand what good Mrs Faulkner sees in it. Thereafter Mr Pittman asks whether it is not basically a matter of being taken seriously at all. A long silence follows, heavy with insight. Eventually I interrupt it by giving the following interpretation: At every new contact there is a fear of being exploited and cheated. Obviously this fear dominates all relationships, including the group's relationship with me. It is possible that I too only use the group to exploit it, that I only want to earn money. The group also fears that behind the participants' interest in each other there are unscrupulous motives. The group confirms this interpretation. Mrs Sinfield and Mrs Sheen nod in agreement and Mr Morgan concludes: 'That is the reason why I have sexual difficulties with my wife. I sense that she feels exploited by me.'

4 Theoretical perspective

What sort of resistance phenomena appear in this session? To begin with both women, Mrs Sinfield and Mrs Sheen, deny their desire for independence and in fact behave in a dependent fashion. This behaviour is recognizable in the helplessness with which they hold the forms in their hands. The conductor first accepts this defence against the desire for independence and replies to the questions in a factual manner. At the same time the information given is designed to help these two participants to become more independent. The housewife still persists in hiding behind her husband. At a conscious level she wants to depend on him, but unconsciously she would like to be independent of him. Both women do the same with the conductor. In front of him they appear dependent and helpless, but in reality they want to free themselves from him. To a large extent, these strivings for independence are still blocked by the defence mechanism of denial. In this initial phase the young aggressive Mr Gage is closer to this crucial theme than are the two women, even though he is very agitated because of it. His strivings for independence, however, fade away in the very moment when another man, Mr Morgan – who in his turn denies his own desire for independence – asks him how he is. Mr Gage's demonstration of independence is stopped by the very question he had conjured up. The question had been provoked by him because his agitation and flushed head indicated insecurity. Basically, he wants the others to care for him, and he is furious when they do not. Therefore, the conflict hinges on desires for independence and on desires for dependence. The desires for independence are represented by the two women and are defended against by the women showing themselves helpless. The desires for dependence are defended against by exhibiting marked independence as the dynamic Mr Gage does.

Intertwined within this independence/dependence conflict there is another conflict, that between sexual impulses and the anxiety that one might infringe upon deeply rooted prohibitions which have been internalized early in life. This conflict has been growing in the group for quite a while. It was defended against by the Morgan-Sinfield couple separating itself from the group. After Mr Gage had seen them together by mere chance, it is no longer possible for the couple to avoid confronting the conflict and dealing with it in the here and now. The defence against the participants' sexual impulses became clear after the conflict had been repressed and certain symptoms appeared surrounded by awkward silences.

The conflict between sexual impulses and prohibitions is further complicated by yet another; that which consists in the concept that sex cannot be experienced on a partnership level, but only as man's and woman's mutual oppression and exploitation. This conflict is expressed mainly by Mrs Sheen, while most of the other group members and especially Mrs Faulkner, defend themselves against it. I attempt to touch upon all three conflicts, but the difficulty for my interpretations to be effective is that the participants use one conflict to defend against the other. A virtual hierarchy of conflicts was reached with specific anxieties pertaining to each of them. Those anxieties related to independence seem to be the most powerful because they are linked to separation and loss of love. They are defended against through denial. The fear of being punished because of infidelity is less strong, but again the fear of being exploited in sexual relationships is more pronounced. In my first interpretation I address myself to the problem of independence/dependence. The group, however, does not pick it up at this point. First another theme moves into the foreground. By reporting on the Sunday excursion, Mr Gage presents the problem of sex to the group. It means that given the continuing resistance against working through the problem of independence/dependence, the group prefers the sexual theme. In its turn this theme also calls for defence because of anxieties about punishment. These anxieties are defended against through repression. One can recognize the repression through the symptoms: Mrs Sheen gets goose-flesh, Mrs Murphy trembles like a leaf, while Mrs Sinfield claims to be having a heart attack and Mrs Faulkner is near to fainting. Obviously, the mention of the excursion led to the anticipation of punishment for having infringed sexual prohibitions. It also triggered off strong desires for sexual gratification. These wishes in their turn raised resistance because the women experience them as submission to the man.

Mr Gage brings the independence/dependence conflict to the foreground once more — which is the original conflict in this group and, in my opinion, the decisive one. From his excluded position Mr Gage attacks the various couples: Mr Morgan and Mrs Sinfield, Mrs Faulkner and the conductor, the group and the conductor. Though the attack expresses his personal resistance to the problem of sex, at the same time it takes the whole group back to the theme 'to be or not to be dependent'. The group in its turn dodges this conflict and picks up the sex theme as the lesser evil.

Thus it becomes clear that parts of what is defended against are always contained in the resistance itself. This is so because the feelings which are defended against, are in their turn used to resist some other feelings. At the beginning of the session it is the women who defend against their wishes for independence simply by denying them. Mrs Faulkner unconsciously takes hold of the same defence mechanism of denial. She declares that her relationship with her partner is good when in actual fact it is encumbered with conflicts of subordination and dominance. The three women who resist the dependence/independence conflict allow, however, the discussion of the sexual theme brought up by Mr Gage's report on the Sunday outing. At first they even experience this theme as a relief. When, however, due to Mr Gage the sexual excitement intensifies, the sexual theme too triggers off anxiety which is followed by corresponding resistance. Unlike the previous defence through denial of the wishes for independence, this resistance uses the defence mechanism of repression. The result is the compromise of bodily symptom formation such as trembling, heartpain and faintness. Mr Gage's next contribution pulls the group again from its attitude of resistance. He confronts the group with its need for dependence. By doing so, he in his turn defends himself against his feelings of envy and jealousy.

In the course of this session it was not yet possible sufficiently to analyse the group's resistance against its wishes for independence. On the other hand, the resistance against clearly satisfactory sex relations and against the desire for being taken seriously has considerably weakened. Though resistance against aspirations for independence was not yet overcome, at least the group had learned to accept sexual desires and the wish to be taken seriously with less anxiety and less resistance than before. This last point means: If I am taken seriously, then I can allow others to help me without having to fear losing my independence because of being helped.

Chapter 7

Transference in psychoanalytic group therapy, exemplified by Group 2

1 Transference by the individual to another individual

Transference is as important in psychoanalytic group therapy as it is in individual psychoanalysis. Piet C. Kuiper is right when he states that transference is the *via regia* of analysis'.[1] It is through transference that past becomes present, the 'then and there' changes into the 'here and now'. Sibling rivalries are especially easily re-enacted in the group through transferences. Triangles such as the relationship between father, mother and child are relived in the relationship with the conductor, the group or another participant. When pathological dyadic relationships are reactivated in the group the transference is not always directed towards the conductor, but often just towards another participant. All these are examples of so-called 'object-relations' transferences. In these transferences the emotions and attitudes the infant originally felt towards a primary object — usually towards mother or father — are transferred to a current object, the possible current object in a group being the conductor, another group member or the group-as-a-whole.

We have already seen examples of such transferences in Chapter 5 when we discussed the mutual hatred between the sexes in Group 1. This hatred revealed itself only after Mr Gage, acting as a 'speaker', managed to transfer his murderous feelings on to the conductor. He was able to express the frustrated child's unconscious hatred towards the not-good-enough mother, and the conductor was experienced by the group as such a mother. Let us recall the scene in which Mr Gage abused the conductor as someone who only sits and grins like a stuffed dummy, pockets money for his silence and so forth. This was a primary hatred common to all participants and directed towards the conductor, though it was concealed by the mutual hatred between men and women. This interpretation was confirmed by Mr Gage recalling: Yes, it was the same once upon a time with his mother and elder sisters as it is now in the group. He feels exactly the same now as he felt at that time.

Other participants who also experienced me as the repressive mother — as for instance did Mrs Sheen — were able to share such a transference. The same person, in this case the same conductor, is, however, a different 'peg' for the different participants' transferences. The 'peg' itself can be a gesture, a certain posture, a certain intonation in speech, a passing facial expression, a certain utterance, a single word and many other things. The transferences of any participant can get 'fixed' on to any of the 'pegs'. A very specific detail can stir up in us intense experiences which we lived through long ago with closely related persons of our childhood. It is especially the unpleasant memories that remain stuck in our unconscious mind without having been worked through. Only after they have been transferred, can these unpleasant experiences become accessible in the here and now and be worked through.

We have seen also in Chapter 5 how the group defended itself against its hatred of the conductor by concealing it behind the mother's hatred for her children. The hatred for the conductor in its turn was covering up the even more unconscious infantile hatred for mother. This hatred appeared in its most intense form in the destructive impulses of Mr Gage. His emotional transferences were especially vehement because he was able, quite directly, to relive within the group his childhood situation with his mother and elder sisters.

Finally, there was too the transference of sexual desires on to the conductor. Mrs Sinfield developed a typical transference love which was revealed through the dream she reported. She was strolling hand-in-hand with the conductor in a meadow full of flowers. Not long after this dream, the group learned how Mr Morgan fell in love with Mrs Sinfield.

2 Group transference

The examples given so far were transferences of an individual to another individual. These transferences occur in the group as well as in individual analysis. The only difference is that in a group there is a far greater choice of 'pegs' for the individual transferences. In addition, there are transference configurations which are quite specific to the group, such as the transference by the group-as-a-whole to the conductor. Whenever all participants share a common unconscious fantasy about the conductor, we speak of a 'group transference'.[2] For instance, this transference can be an attitude of oral expectation which means that the conductor, like a mother, is expected to give nourishment. A group that has no particular topic for discussion can find itself very quickly in such a situation. Once this position is reached, other needs as well − such as the need for contact, tenderness, touching, warmth and security − seek gratification. The type of relationship we then witness is the classic relationship between mother and child. In the psychoanalytic literature of the last two decades or so a great deal has been written about this relationship. It suffices to mention the work of René A. Spitz[3] on the first year of life, that of Donald W. Winnicott[4] on the facilitating environment and the supportive function of the mother, and the work of Margret S. Mahler.[5] The latter distinguishes a stage of symbiotic fusion between mother and child, as well as a stage of separation from this symbiosis. In Chapter 10 we shall return to this important stage of early development.

The following is an example of oral expectation taken from Group 2. Like Group 1, Group 2 also consisted of four women and four men. They worked together over a period of three years through 171 sessions of 100 minutes éach. As in Group 1 in this group too there was tense expectation in the first session. In order not to let the tension mount excessively, I gave the interpretation that the unknown situation caused anxiety. It was interesting to observe that this group also attempted to broach the theme 'man and woman' as a means of avoiding the real issue which was their dependence on me. One of the first contributions came from Ralph, a 25-year-old student of electrical engineering. He had serious problems with his studies, was insecure in his social life, and suffered from grandiose fantasies along with deep feelings of inferiority. On an unconscious level he was attached intimately to his prohibiting mother. His father was a labourer who drank and did not inspire the youngster by his example. Ralph started by saying: 'I did not expect to find so many women here'. He thought that because they get recognition, women should be more able than men to cope with their difficulties. One of the four women reacted: No, no, that is not so at all. Women also have their problems, though they might be different problems from those he has as a man. Another woman promptly suggested that the group should perhaps try to look more closely at the men's problems.

Further contributions continued to move round the man/woman antithesis. Meanwhile the atmosphere was saturated with some kind of great expectation directed towards the conductor. I interpreted this situation by saying that obviously the participants found a common theme for discussion, namely the familiar question of the differences between man and woman. Although this is an important topic, it seemed to me that it covered up other difficulties which were prevalent in the here and now.

After this interpretation the discussion was led by a workman who tended to intellectualize and later on dropped out from the group. With his help the group managed for a while to defend against its oral problem. Eventually, the theme was picked up and worked through vigorously thanks to two women who felt increasingly oppressed by the intellectualizing workman. One of the women, Mary, a 26-year-old married accountant, blushed when she spoke of her constant vomiting. Much later it was discovered that this harrowing symptom concealed her insatiable greed and destructive aggression as well as the anxiety caused by these impulses and the defence against the anxiety itself. Mary was born out of wedlock and brought up by her single mother who grossly neglected her. Mary did not know her father. When she was six years old, a step-father came into the family who could not develop any relationship with the child. He demanded all mother's care and attention for himself, thus further increasing Mary's deprivations. After Mary had revealed the symptom of which she was so ashamed, Louise, a 28-year-old unmarried nursery school teacher, was able to join in the discussion. She had sought therapy because of her depressive disorder and her tendency to misuse drugs. She too was born out of wedlock, grew up with mother and mother's parents and she did not know her father either. Louise started by saying that the gist of the matter was to admit frankly to each other what one really felt. She centred all her hopes on Dr Kutter. Surely, help will come from him. By saying this she expressed the group's attitudes of expectation. This attitude is called by W.R. Bion[6] the basic assumption of dependence. This is the prevalent attitude when the group expects everything from the conductor and considers itself utterly unable to achieve anything. Having given up their identity to a certain extent, the individual participants merge into each other. Unconsciously they make themselves into one 'big' infant who is totally dependent on the conductor. The latter is experienced as the all-powerful mother who is incessantly dishing out nourishment. There is a magic expectation that the conductor will give them food, security, warmth, all the things they missed in childhood and for which they secretly longed ever since. In this situation the conductor represents 'something like a group divinity'.[7] The deep-seated problems Mary and Louise had, fitted in well with this attitude. These two women were the ones who felt most directly the group's position of unconscious expectation and managed to verbalize it most clearly.

After some initial hesitation, and having swallowed his pride, a male participant soon joined them. This was Albert, a 30-year-old businessman, married, with two children. He suffered from a phobic fear of dying from lack of air and because no one came to his rescue. He used to be seized by this fear while sitting in his car in traffic jams and also in the railway when the carriage was at a standstill. Although he grew up in good middle-class conditions, his mother was not able to respond adequately to his needs in infancy. Therefore, when he became a young boy he could not develop any basic trust towards other people. Albert expressed a strong need to be protected and supported by the conductor. In fact, he demanded that I should give him a sort of certificate he would carry on him. The paper should state the name of the sedative injection he is to be given immediately in case of an anxiety attack. The attitude of oral expectation was shared by most participants in this group. They experienced the conductor as an ideal mother who satisfied their needs. Due to the conductor's unavoidable failures, in the course of further developments in the group this view led eventually to reactions of disappointment.

The group experienced me not only as a mother, but in a later phase also as a father. In the case of Mary and Louise the father was missing. In the case of Ralph the father was weak, insecure, failed professionally and went down the drain because of excessive drinking. Albert's father, though professionally successful, was downright damaging. He not only did not support the son, but harmed him in that he failed to prevent him from hurting himself. (As a five-year-old boy Albert was sitting in the child's seat on his father's bicycle. He put a foot in the spokes of the front wheel, thus severely injuring all five toes.) The other participants of Group 2 had similar experiences even though somewhat less traumatic. They suffered from depressions, lack of energy, unrelatedness and had problems with their work. These symptoms concealed anxieties of being disappointed by others – such as the marriage partner or friends – and now, in the transference situation, by the conductor. These fears were justified in that their idealized expectations were exaggerated and therefore unlikely to be fulfilled.

3 Family transference and idealizing transference

If we compare both groups, we find characteristic differences in what is transferred. The difference in transferences led eventually to quite definite and different structures in the two groups. The participants with 'classical' neuroses in Group 1 experienced me as a clearly defined father or mother figure, whom one loves or hates and by whom one feels loved or hated, but with whom one can always talk. In contrast, the members of Group 2 experienced me as an ideal figure endowed with magic qualities. In the group one can shield oneself from this figure by merging into each other, thus partly giving up one's own boundaries. At the same time one longs for magic healing coming from this figure. Concrete family situations – as the participants had experienced them in childhood – came to form the configuration in Group 1. In other words, family transferences[8] took place in which some participants experienced me as father, while others relived in me their mother or siblings. In Group 2, on the other hand, an idealizing transference occurred which was shared by all. This is the same idealizing transference Heinz Kohut[9] described in the context of individual analysis. The conductor represents an ideal object of paternal or maternal type. This object is all-powerful, has inexhaustible strength, reads the participants' needs from their eyes, and is in complete empathy with each of them. Naturally, one falls in love with this grossly overvalued object. The wish is to become one with it (merger transference) or to see it exactly as grandiose as oneself (alter-ego or twinship transference). It is also possible that one would like to see oneself mirrored in it. This object should reflect all that one longs for, hopes for and all that one desires (mirror transference). If the conductor responds to these expectations, then the participants feel accepted, appreciated and strengthened and make great progress in therapy. If the conductor does not meet these expectations, then disappointments are bound to set in. Reactions of depression, resignation and hopelessness will ensue. These reactions have to be worked through thoroughly otherwise the group process comes to a grinding halt. Without a certain degree of idealization of its conductor the group cannot make any progress. The conductor should be able to establish an atmosphere which allows the participants to place their trust and confidence in him. As we will see in greater detail in Chapter 14, the conductor can induce this trust only by following the group process throughout with the greatest possible concentration. From time to time he has to indicate that he understands what are the issues. Such communications are experienced by the participants as the acknowledgment of their achievements.

Chapter 8

The struggle with authority. Subsequent course of the group process in Group 2

1 The fight for the father

As in Group 1, so in Group 2 the process centred for a long time around the participants' relationship with their mother. The only difference was that in Group 2 the mother was seen in an extraordinarily ideal light — corresponding to an idealizing transference. It became increasingly clear, however, that the participants' symptoms covered up a general feeling of being abandoned. This feeling was especially strong during the conductor's holidays. Ralph retreated into himself, Louise took more drugs than usual. Albert's car and railway phobia worsened and Mary's vomiting intensified. The other members who joined the group later suffered from headaches and other physical complaints. After the conductor's return, participants still felt lonely and forsaken. The manifest depression of a female participant, who dropped out because she could no longer tolerate feeling abandoned, weighed heavily on the group. So did another female patient who temporarily took the place of the former. This member could not cope with the real separation from her mother after she had moved house. The intellectualizing worker showed his emotions for the first time when mourning his grandmother who had just died. It was the dream of another participant — in which empty tables and a starving child appeared — which, once interpreted, revealed what was missing in the group: a mother who lovingly cares for her children as well as a father who gives security and protection. Only many sessions later Ralph — the student with fantasies of grandeur and inferiority complexes — managed to link his anxieties in social life with his father having denied him the help he now was looking for in the group. He started with a dream about a maned lion who protects his cubs. Ralph remembered how different his father had been towards him. Now all participants saw clearly that a reliable father figure was missing. We know from psychoanalysis that a reliable father figure is essential for an individual's development and that its absence leaves more or less serious disorders behind. As the third person alongside mother and child, the father protects the child from an overpowerful mother. The dangers are that such a mother might take possession of the child, sap its strength and be unable to let it go. A mother might behave like that if she, for instance, unconsciously uses the child as the substitute for her unloved partner. If the father does not protect it, the child will not be able to free itself from mother's clutching embrace.[1] Moreover, it is the father who wakes up the child from sleep[2] and, finally, he is also its language teacher and legislator.[3] Through its struggle and identification with the father, the child is able to internalize these paternal functions bit by bit and to become independent. Therefore, these paternal functions, and their subsequent internalization, are the precondition for the child's separation from the symbiosis with the mother. Even when he is actually absent, the father has a 'potential presence'[4] in the mother-child relationship. Also in the group it is of great therapeutic importance to experience this 'potential presence'. 'On the way towards a fatherless society'[5] we find a special form of severe neurotic disturbances characteristic of a specific personality structure with identity disorder.[6]

The tragic consequences of a disturbed relationship with father were revealed in Ralph's life. Around the fiftieth session, when the father problem was at the centre of the group's work, the group asked whether it was not better to grow up without a father than with such fathers as Ralph and Albert had. Such a bad relationship as Ralph had with his father is experienced as shameful as well as overburdening and not a help at all. Ralph's father was an alcoholic and made him feel ashamed because of that. Albert's father had unconscious aggressive impulses against him. He harmed Albert in a concrete form like Laius once harmed Oedipus when he left him out on the mountainside. He did so because he feared that once he grew up, the child would damage him. According to tradition – and in Sophocles' tragedy *Oedipus Rex* – the prophecy came true when Oedipus unknowingly slayed his own father. In a common fantasy of the group, the father became the wolf who threatens the seven kids. One can protect oneself against him only by hiding in the chest. In Mary's case this fear of the father had also a specifically incestuous significance: when drunk her step-father had attempted to seduce her several times.

2 Vengeance on the disappointing father

Because such a father does not give one any support, one hates and also despises him. At the same time one cannot help feeling guilty and sympathetic towards him. These feelings of guilt and sympathy are defended against through repression and symptom formation – such as, for instance, Albert's phobic anxiety. Later on, however, these feelings became manifest in the relationship to the conductor, and were clearly expressed by Ralph. The group was looking for effective leadership even at the risk of being patronized. A consistent interpretation technique with precise formulations was needed to help participants understand their wish for a strong leader and to find their own way. The fear of losing the 'leader', and the anxiety that the conductor might be too weak, reappeared time and time again. The fear was worked through by constantly interpreting the transference, reconstructing childhood experiences and by linking current group dynamics with past events in individual participants' lives. The causative childhood situation had to be relived directly in the group, yet without the 'here and now' being a perfect replica of the original situation. Soon after Group 2 started, participants unconsciously began to fear that I could beat them up (eighth session) or let them down (ninth session), as once the father did when they were children. The real struggle with the problematic fathers began only after the equally threatening mother-child relationship had been worked through – approximately from the fiftieth to the eightieth session. The struggle-with-father theme was introduced by Louise. She started by leading a taxi-driver on: first she promised to go with him on a trip, then she changed her mind. Her behaviour was a straightforward, though unconscious retaliation for her father's failure. The consequent guilt feelings were recognizable from Louise's increased drug intake and Mary's intensified vomiting. Albert's compulsions worsened. Now they were directed against his own children and later on against the conductor. Finally all members of the group shared the common fantasy of taking revenge on the weak father who disappointed them. This fantasy turned up in the ninetieth session which had started with a seemingly trifling discussion about cars. Then one member mentioned that he nearly crashed into a car. Later on someone recalled a car parked in front of the house. Ralph's association was next: he had serious difficulties with his professor who did not help him with his diploma thesis. Albert promptly suggested: 'Tell him at last what you think of him!' After Ralph had rejected this suggestion, a heated debate developed among the men. They could not understand how anybody would want to have children. After all, children had nothing but difficulties in life and there was nobody to stand by and help them. A male participant ran to Albert's support and another to Ralph's support. It was a scene of brothers fighting under my very eyes. This scene can only be explained by the fact that in their unconscious fantasy I was the father. In their perception this father either was simply non-existent — as in the case of Mary and Louise, or he was totally inadequate and weak — as in Ralph's case, or he was so threatening that one would prefer to steer clear of him — as in Albert's case. All of them unconsciously experienced the father as being struck dead, deceased or buried.

3 Symbolic killing of the father and reparation

In a later phase of the group process, the father came alive again. Mary remembered how her step-father forbade her to go out and how he broke her beloved flute in her presence, and other equally awful scenes. When a father who has been destroyed previously is resuscitated in this way, then we can say, using Melanie Klein's words, that the murderous brothers and sisters, led by their guilt feelings, and in a gesture of reparation call back to life the murdered father.[7]

The processes which took place in Group 2 correspond to general psychological patterns and sooner or later occur in all groups. Leon Grinberg, Marie Langer and Emil Rodrigué, who based their work mainly on Melanie Klein, write:[8]

> Essential changes in the group's basic structure occur — and this is the way in which a group can be therapeutically effective — when the patients are free to express their hostility and by doing so they discover that the consequences are not as fatal as they had feared; furthermore, when they re-live their guilt — which includes the love that opposes hatred — at the same time they see the possibility of repairing the damage they believe they have caused; and, finally, when the therapist gives them the right interpretations at the right time.

All this was written as early as 1960 in the first edition of their book which was not widely read at that time. Even today after more than five years' experience in therapeutic work with groups I could not agree more with the points these authors make.

A further process of 'remembering, repeating and working-through'[9] followed, during which Group 2 managed to re-enact negative aspects of the father relationship by transferring those feelings on to me. At the same time the participants experienced the fact that I could stand up to their attacks. Feelings of guilt followed these attacks, leading to a temporary worsening of symptoms: Ralph had twinges of pain in his heart, Mary's vomiting intensified again, and Albert had anxious dreams. Once the guilt feelings were worked through, the group was again able to look at the positive aspects of my person. Then recollections of their fathers' good sides followed with which they identified. The precondition for this selective identification with their fathers' positive aspects was that I had been able to observe and admit my own inattentiveness and moments of indifference in some phases of the group process, and in relation to one or the other participant. These admissions allowed the group to work through the negative experiences I had unwittingly generated. Thereafter participants were able to establish a better relationship with me. These clarifications around my person had to be conducted with total openness. In the end this process enabled some participants to sort out their relationships with their fathers in real life to whom wholesale blame had been attached up to then. Louise clarified her relationship with her own father and Mary with her step-father.

A participant who joined the group at a later stage found it especially difficult to cope with rejection by her father. She was Gisela, a 29-year-old technical assistant. She had already had a hundred hours group therapy in another town in northern Germany. Apparently the conductor of that group did not follow psychoanalytic principles and had offered himself as a real significant person. Due to my more detached psychoanalytic attitude, Gisela felt that I rejected her and, just like her boss, did not appreciate her. The boss himself was a transference figure towards whom she could express her dissatisfaction with her own father. More or less the same happened to another new member of Group 2, William, a 31-year-old manager. He joined the group after having had 200 hours individual therapy. Nevertheless, both Gisela and William — thanks to their previous experience of therapy — managed to settle down quickly in the group and thus contribute to its progress. Gisela dreamed that she murdered her father — the dream was about an open coffin with father lying squeezed into it. Mary's step-father appeared to her hobbling along on one leg, while the other leg was deformed. After these two dreams were reported, the group all of a sudden realized that it wanted to get rid of me (164th session). At the same time there was anxiety as to whether both parties would be able to survive the separation. Having overcome their separation anxieties, the participants started to be able to experience each other as real people, to help each other effectively, and to do without me as a conductor. Also their relationships in real life began to change, or to put it more precisely, they began to differentiate themselves from their fathers. Mary arranged a meeting with her step-father and confronted him. Even if it did not bring a reconciliation, at least this encounter helped to correct her fantasies about him. The other members of the group also shared in this process. Feeling the group's protection, Albert decided to have cosmetic surgery on his crippled foot. Through the person of the conductor he actually managed to make peace with his father. Mary's vomiting kept on recurring almost until the end of the group, but then it petered out and vanished completely. The symptom ceased once its sexual as well as its aggressive component had been worked through. The causes of this tenacious symptom were not only anxiety and fear of punishment, but above all hatred and desire for vengeance for the gross neglect by the father and his irresponsible behaviour. Mary's vomiting was always preceded by swallowing food hastily. Her immediate experience of nourishment was that of something which had to be spat out rather than to be digested.

For long stretches the group did with me what Mary unconsciously did with food: The group had taken in my interpretations for a while, but it spat them out shortly afterwards. At the same time with the steady improvement of Mary's symptom, the group as a whole was approaching the point of overcoming the struggle with their fathers. This fight, carried over from dim and distant childhood into adulthood, never ceased to prey on the participants' nerves. Once they were relieved of it, they found new ways of turning to their partners.

Chapter 9

The group process: each individual participates in shared events

1 The group process seen through the three-layers-model

The prominence given to some individuals, such as to the dynamic Mr Gage in Group 1 or Mary, Louise and Ralph in Group 2, might have given the impression that my kind of group therapy is a therapy of the individual in the group which would mean that I adhere to the theoretical model described in the first section of Chapter 3. This is, however, not the case. I will now attempt to show how I see the individual's participation in the shared group process. For me the group is a system, a substratum or 'matrix' as S.H. Foulkes[1] terms it. This system is composed of several people and, as has already been pointed out in Chapter 3, is something more than the sum of its parts. Again in Foulkes's terminology,[2] all parts together form a so-called 'network' of relationships which has a quite definite structure. Often one can discern this structure from the participants' seating arrangement. For instance, for long stretches during the period of struggle between the sexes in Group 1 a block of four men sat facing an equally large one of women. In another phase of the group process, the dynamic Mr Gage sat as a polar opposite to me while the other group members sat between us to his left and right forming a buffer zone.

However, it is not always possible to recognize clearly the prevalent group structure on the basis of the seating arrangement. Most of the time we have to rely purely on our psychoanalytic perception of group processes. Under constant training and supervision, this perception develops progressively and is refined by experience. Testing our psychoanalytic perception against theoretical models will also help us to find our way in the wealth and variety of group processes. If we follow the first model, the therapy of the individual in the group, we will see the individual developing intensive and long-lasting transferences towards the conductor and towards other group members. These transferences are by no means weaker than those encountered in individual analysis. All that we need to do is not to overlook them.[3]

To understand, observe and interpret the group process according to the second model – the therapy of the group through the group with the individual's participation – is a far more complex and demanding task.[4] The process starts with the structure predetermined through the selection of participants. If we observe the group process closely, we will recognize that it runs through a more or less regular succession of different phases. We have already considered this succession in relation to the Freudian stages of psycho-sexual development and Erikson's eight stages of man. In addition, there is my own three-layers-model which I presented in an earlier publication. This model coincides partly with a classification by Foulkes,[5] at the time unknown to me, as well as with another classification by Heigl-Evers[6] which was published later. Previously, Wolfgang Loch had applied a similar model to brief individual therapy.[7]

The three layers in my model are:

1 The surface layer of the conscious, actual interactions, that is to say, the layer of group dynamics. Here we are dealing, among other things, with the participants' social role.
2 The layer of the transference and counter-transference relationships. Here the struggle with the parental figures of the past takes place. In their unconscious fantasies participants relive each significant person of the past in the person of the conductor around whom the fights flare-up.
3 The deep unconscious layer of the anaclitic regression of the group to which the analyst is corresponding in a specific diatrophic attitude.[8] In this layer the group looks for the conductor's support, but it also goes through processes which are as strongly destructive as they are idealizing. We will see examples of these processes in Group 3.

If we introduce the dimension of time into this three-layers-model, then we can figure out a variety of sequences. A very typical sequence is one in which the group process starts with current conflicts. By continually working through resistances and defences the process penetrates further and further back into conflicts of the past as far back as those of early childhood and then slowly going through later stages of development. I myself have experienced such a sequence as a participant of an experimental group conducted by Erich Lindemann.[9] With some periodic intervals this group met for more than ten years. The same, rather typical sequence also occurred in Group 1 whose members mostly suffered from classical neuroses.

2 The narcissism-theory of the group

In Group 2 where most of the participants suffered from narcissistic personality disorders, the sequence of events was different. Here an increasing idealization of the therapist developed and was followed by an idealization of the group. The idealization of the therapist corresponds to a reactivation of the parents' idealization by the infant, while the group's idealization is a projection of the ideal parts of the participants' selves. The narcissism theory of the group helps one to understand a group in which the conductor shows traits of an idealized parental figure and the group itself shows the features of a grandiose self which is shared by all. The phenomenon of the grandiose self is known through Heinz Kohut's description of the individual analysis of patients with narcissistic personality disorders.[10] Such a narcissistic group is highly vulnerable in its self-value, easily hurt and disappointed. It might react to what it feels to be offences and humiliations with temporary symptoms of disintegration or with so-called narcissistic rage.[11]

3 The segment-theory of the group

Quite apart from the fact of whether most participants suffer from classical neuroses or from narcissistic personality disorders, it is always the individual histories that contribute to form the group process. Each individual constitutes a segment of the group process. In the end the sum of all segments forms a 'specific internal structure', that is to say a 'form' or 'culture' that has its own well-defined rules. This common structure changes all the time to the same extent as its individual segments change. Such a structure which, so to speak, flows through the individual contributions, in its turn drives the individual through quite definite phases and into quite definite positions within the structure. These positions will depend on the conflict the individual brings into the group. For instance, a participant whose fixation is at the oral stage, will 'enter' with particular vigour the group process when it reaches the oral layer of mother-child relationship. A female group member whose fixation is at the genital stage will participate most actively when the group reaches the level of genital conflicts.

In Group 1 all participants, except Mr Gage, managed to participate in the group process to a nearly equal extent. All of them more or less suffered from classical neuroses, the causes of which were genital conflicts shared by all. Also in Group 2 each participant contributed an approximately equal segment to the whole. Nevertheless, as the segments were of different kinds, they led to a 'specific group structure as a result of the personality structures entering into it'.[12]

Having seen the various possibilities of a group process, let us look again at our layers-model. An abstract and merely theoretical construct of the group process can be drawn graphically as follows (see Fig. 9.1). We arrange the three layers as three concentric half-circles. Each segment represents a participant's individual personality structure. The half-circle as a whole represents in its turn a cross-section of an ongoing longitudinal process. Which segment is contributed at any one time depends on the individual as well as on the current structure of the group process. The idea is that a participant's segment fits like a key the lock of the group's current structure. In his book *Die Zweierbeziehung* (*The Dyadic Relationship*) Jörg Willi beautifully described these processes as they apply to married couples.[13] As married couples can act in unison, harmonious couples — which means subgroups — emerge also in groups. One part of the pair fits the other exactly. Such a perfect matching of two parts can be observed when a new member enters into an already established group structure. His predecessor has left a gap behind. The newcomer can fill this gap, provided that his personality structure fits into the group structure in the same way as that of his predecessor. If this is not the case, then the individual segments begin to displace each other. These displacements perturb the group process over a lengthy period of time and thus hamper the therapeutic process.

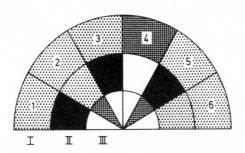

Figure 9.1 Six group members' participation, represented as segments of a cross-section of the group process. I Social interactions layer; II transference layer; III deep unconscious layer (regression).

At the time of this particular cross-section, participant 1 finds himself in layer II which is the transference layer. The same applies to participants 3 and 5. On the other hand, very little is happening at the level of social interactions (layer I). Moreover, participants 2 and 5 begin to submerge into layer III, while participant 4 can find his place only outside layers II and III, namely by carrying a social role. Given this particular cross-section of the group process, transference interpretations would 'hit' only participants 1, 3 and 5, without reaching the other three participants.

If we manage to draw such an outline for each session, then we will be in a position to follow the progress over time of the individual participants (segments) as well as of the group-as-a-whole (half-circle).

4   Four levels of transference in the layers-model

Let us recall that the participants of Group 1 suffered predominantly from classical neuroses, and those of Group 2 mostly from narcissistic personality disorders. Therefore, we are compelled to divide layer II into at least two sub-layers, namely:

a   the level of transference processes in classical neuroses;
b   the level of the narcissistic transference and the mobilization of parts of one's own grandiose self.

We have to add further two sub-levels which have not yet been discussed:

c   the level of the so-called 'splitting transferences'. These are characterized by the fact that the relationships with the significant person, mostly the mother, is split into two opposite parts, one perfectly good and the other only bad. In Group 1 Mr Gage's transferences showed such a split. In Group 3, which we will meet in Chapter 10, 'splitting transferences' occurred with great frequency. They were the rule rather than the exception.
d   The level of 'psychotic transferences' or 'transference psychosis'. On this level the boundaries between individual participants are blurred. In a group composed exclusively of psychotics, we should expect such a structure to appear in its purest form. According to André Green,[14] hidden in each of us there is a more or less distinct so-called 'psychotic core'. This core can be mobilized if the group process lasts long enough and penetrates deep enough to reach it.

Summing up, we have the following subdivision of layer II:

a the layer of transference neurosis;
b the layer of narcissistic transferences with their idealizations;
c the layer of the splitting transferences;
d the layer of psychotic transferences or transference psychosis.

With this detailed layers-model in front of us we will be able to determine at any point in time how the cross-section of the group process is structured. In Group 1 all participants contributed segments to layer IIa. Mr Gage added to the group process further elements corresponding to sublayers IIb and IIc. Participants' individual segments in Group 2 formed together a structure prevalently on the level of narcissistic transferences (sub-layer IIb). If we now imagine our layers-model in a time sequence, then a half-cylindrical structure would emerge composed of the segments of the individual participants reaching different depths. Graphically it would look approximately like Figure 9.2:

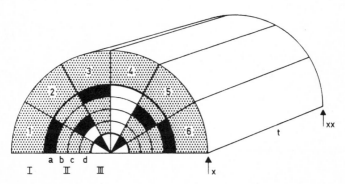

Figure 9.2 Illustration of six group members' participation, represented as segments in two cross-sections in the course of the group process. t = time; x = cross-section one; xx = cross-section two

The group process is represented as a half-cylinder. In cross-section one participants 1, 3 and 6 are located in sub-layer IIa which corresponds to the classical neuroses, while participant 5 develops a narcissistic transference and participant 2 a splitting transference. In addition, participants 2 and 5 occupy also the deep unconscious layer of the anaclitic regression (see Chapter 9.1). From cross-section one up to cross-section two the level of transference can remain the same or it can change.

Obviously both models can be extended to become a full circle and, including the time dimension, a cylinder. This device can conveniently represent a group process with a greater number of segments, i.e. of participants. With the help of this graphic representation one can record the position of each individual participant in the group process at any point in time one chooses. Successive cross-sections can help to discover possible displacements in the intensity and level of participation in group events.

5   Initial phase, main phase and end phase of the group process

The distinction already mentioned between initial, main and end phases within the group process offers us a further frame of reference. The initial phase corresponds to the introduction of the treatment.[15] In this phase the principal themes are the participants' motives, their time investment and the fee which is paid to the analyst. Once these questions have been discussed, and settled, the process characteristic of that particular group begins to unfold. The precondition for it is that the conductor refrains from premature interpretations that would disturb the development of the specific group process.

In the main phase of the group process the specific structure of the group has already been established. This structure can be hysterical as, for instance, in the case of Group 1, or narcissistic as in the case of Group 2. In this phase there is 'remembering, repeating and working through'.[16] The group works through resistances and transferences develop and are interpreted. In this main phase there is considerable danger of acting out and participants might attempt to cope with painful memories not in the group, but outside the group. This was partly the case with Group 1 when Mr Morgan invited Mrs Sinfield on their Sunday outing. On the other hand, if such an outside activity is brought back to the group — even if it is mentioned only by one participant — then it can help to promote the group process as happened in Group 2.

We will deal with the end phase of the group process in Chapter 16, taking as our frame of reference Freud's publication of 1937 under the memorable title *Analysis Terminable and Interminable*.[17]

Chapter 10
Early mother-child relationship in the group: split into good and bad

1 Destruction and reparation

We have already seen in Chapter 5 what an important role the early dyadic relationship plays in psychoanalytic group therapy. The hatred against the strict and rejecting mother appeared clearly in the relationship between the conductor and the participants of Group 1. The former was experienced as a kind of sphinx, a 'supermother' who, though she knows everything, lets the participants solve riddles which are difficult to decipher. 'He sits there like a Buddha!' This was the feeling Mr Gage expressed about the conductor's posture. Group members feel dwarfed and shrink into insignificance beside him. They think he is full of strength, an inexhaustible divinity who, in order to keep them dependent, gives them none of that strength. This idea leads to primitive hatred and impulses to destroy the mother, to cut her into pieces, robbing her of her contents. Such wishes are followed by anxiety, feelings of guilt and a need for reparation. The destructive personality parts are projected to the outside in order to defend oneself against anxiety and feelings of guilt.

This is an entirely archaic relationship to a mother who is experienced as utterly malevolent, so much so that such a thoroughly bad object can no longer be felt as a coherent person, but only as a part, such as the breast, head, belly, vagina. Given this experience, the participants might lose their boundaries as individuals, thus becoming dependent parts of the archaic mother imago, entirely at her mercy. During such a far-reaching regression the participants themselves are no longer able to test reality which they perceive only through the conductor's eyes.

The feelings that prevail among group members are primitive fears of losing their identity, of being swallowed and engulfed by the archaic object. These fears are often defended against by aggressive behaviour directed at an enemy the group members find or create outside the group. Another defence is simply to take flight from the danger which they experience as terrifying. The defence can also appear in the form of an exaggerated clinging to later conflicts – such as conflicts between the sexes – which serve to cover up earlier more fundamental conflicts. This was the case in Group 1 until the ninety-ninth session. As we shall see, in that session there was a sudden turn of events triggered off by Mr Gage's attacks. A violent struggle between men and women had been going on for several weeks. The group seemed to have fallen into a deep pit. It became totally helpless, paralysed and unable to free itself. At first I was experienced as an impotent and useless father who, instead of running to his children's rescue, looks on while an evil foe destroys them. After I had talked about this scene calmly and coherently, the group began to see me as someone obviously capable of standing up to these murderous attacks. This new view allowed the group to calm down and in the next session, the hundredth, the theme was continued. Again Mr Gage was raging against me as well as against the other participants. He complained because of lack of support and attacked Mrs Sheen in particular. Speaking in a hurtful manner, he blamed her for having no imagination, for destroying everything in the group, for keeping him down and not letting him grow. She burst into tears and while sobbing convulsively, she left the room.

After this scene it became clear that Mr Gage projected his own destructive aggression on to poor Mrs Sheen and tried to fight it in her. Once his projection had been properly interpreted and he managed to take it back, he suddenly discovered that fantasy can be something enormously valuable. For instance, it can help one to free oneself from dependence on a person whom one experiences as ominously threatening. He remembered how as a small boy he once played on the rubbish dump. With objects he found there he constructed a small work of art out of his fantasy. He was very proud of it, but mother and sisters radically devalued his creation.

Once the struggle between Mr Gage and Mrs Sheen was clarified as being the repetition of the struggle between mother and son, the other participants were able to contribute similar experiences. Now they ventured to go further, using their fantasy and creative thinking. This imaginative activity increased steadily and was facilitated by the conductor who took it up and kept on interpreting it. This process – creativity alternating with interpretations – helped participants to free themselves from the archaic mother who had immobilized them.

2 Envy of the mother who possesses everything

There are also phases, however, when the group feels well, as if on the lap of a good mother. It becomes passive and experiences the conductor, and particularly his interpretations, as disturbing. During such a phase the group's unconscious wish is to suck again at the breast and above all to be protected from interferences. These harmonious phases are regularly interrupted by the revival of the not-good-enough mother who is experienced as frustrating and evil. On an oral level she neglects one or even lets one starve; on an anal level she oppresses one's expansive aspirations; on a genital level she wants either to seduce or to castrate one. In any event she is experienced as an existential threat.

Such feelings set in very easily in the group because each group member has to content himself with an eighth or ninth of the 'cake' (depending on the number of participants), while in reality everyone would like to have the whole attention all of the time. Unlike in individual analysis, no one participant is the analyst's only child. Far from it, group members are sevenlets, eightlets and ninelets of one and the same mother, and that at one and the same time.

If the relationship of the whole group to the conductor is that towards a mother, then envy will be the driving force for long stretches of the group process. Though feelings of envy are not always directly recognizable, one can sense them in the 'poisoned' atmosphere and the tendency to devalue the conductor's interpretations. Also the solidarity among participants can be destroyed, when their envy is directed towards each other and is bottled up within themselves. At times, however, group members are very aware of their envy. For instance, they might envy the house in which the therapist lives, the neighbourhood in which the house is located, the furnishings of his consulting room, his clothes and not least his income from the fees he receives. It is important to recognize the envy in communications about this sort of detail concerning the conductor and to work them through. Only after this transference dynamic becomes sufficiently clear, is it possible to understand the pertinent prehistory of the envy and its origin in a frustrating mother-child relationship.

3 Splitting processes in Group 3

In phases of deep regression not only are feelings of envy mobilized, but also parts of the self are split. To be more precise, what happens is that parts of the self are externalized from one's own person into the group or into the person of the conductor. If this occurs, the conductor is no longer experienced as another subject, but as part of oneself. If such parts are aspects of the conscience, then the conductor will represent the personified conscience, the externalized superego. Participants with narcissistic personality disorders in Group 2 experienced the conductor as an idealized parent imago, the ideal mother or the ideal father which means that they were able to idealize a whole person. In Group 3, which will now be introduced, actual parts of the group members, and more exactly their own ideals, were projected on to the conductor. I call Group 3 the 'students' group' because, in contrast to Groups 1 and 2, it consisted mainly of young participants, most of whom were university students or had dropped out from the university. The first session of this group was more dramatic than any other group session I had ever experienced before. John, a 26-year-old clerk and a dropout from philosophy studies, suggests that the group members should perhaps introduce themselves to each other. Elsbeth, a 28-year-old assistant medical doctor, interrupts him in the middle of the sentence in order to present a highly topical problem of hers: she asks whether she should divorce or not. Other members also mention problems they have with their partners. Marian, a 22-year-old student, member of a Marxist-Leninist group, joins in and reports on a triangular relationship between her, her boy-friend and his friend, a man who exploits him. Evelyn, a 27-year-old graphic designer, who now studies education as a second career, feels neglected by her husband and brings her tense relationship with him into the group. The other five members, out of a total of nine in the group, though they say nothing to begin with, follow the whirling events with visible alarm. Bill flushes. He is a 30-year-old tradesman, the eldest member of this group. Eric, a 25-year-old student of music, glances at me time and again with wide open, anxious eyes. Obviously he hopes to find in me a quiet pole against the group's turbulent ado. The excitement increases as Elsbeth, the assistant doctor, speaks openly about her lack of orgasm and poses the question whether this failure stems from her or her husband. At first it remains unclear whether she is asking the conductor, the participants or herself. As no answer is forthcoming from any side, she turns to one particular participant. This is Grace, a 25-year-old accountant, who noticeably winces at Elsbeth's question. Lucy, a 23-year-old girl, who sits next to Grace, reacts in the same way. She too is startled and clearly hurt. Wilfrid, a 25-year-old mechanic who dropped out from his studies of physics, intervenes in a protective fashion which enables Grace to speak. She did not come here because of sexual problems, but because of her mother who never cared for her. When Grace was a child, mother always left her on her own and went out to work. So she has become an outsider, cut off from her environment. She is often closeted in her room and people find her behaviour odd. During Grace's communication the group remains calm for a short while, but soon after it relapses into the initial bustle in which no participant could talk without being interrupted and one could only make out snatches of communications.

4 The borderline-theory of the group

Following Leon Grinberg, Marie Langer and Emilio Rodrigué,[1] we can say that this first session of Group 3 was characterized by so-called 'schizoid' processes. They are processes of splitting, through which participants, so to speak, fall to 'pieces' which are either entirely good or entirely bad. In the first session outlined above we could see the good parts appearing in the persons of Grace and Wilfrid, while Elsbeth and Marian appeared to be outright evil and destructive. These good and bad parts originate from individual group members who unconsciously 'delegate' them to the group. In other words, they project these split-off parts on to other group members. What appears in front of us corresponds to the so-called 'tranference-split'. In Chapter 9, when presenting the division of our model into sub-layers, we discussed this 'transference-split' (sublayer IIc). Following Otto F. Kernberg,[2] the disorders of members of Group 3 — which were even more severe than the disorders found in Group 2 — can be placed into the category of a so-called 'borderline personality organization'. Such a personality organization is on the border between neurosis and psychosis and is characterized by so-called ego-weakness, deficient impulse control, that is to say only limited ability to channel instinctual drives towards social goals, remarkably low threshold for tolerating anxiety and heightened vulnerability and hurtfulness. The ego-weakness is due to the unresolved relationship patterns which, instead of being integrated into the personality, have been split off and are constantly ready to be projected on to other people. The early childhood relationship between mother and child was too bad to be integrated into the ego. Such an extremely bad relationship can arise simply from lack of maternal care or it can be that the supposedly caring mother experienced the child as part of herself. Whatever the reasons, the environment was not sufficiently loving to facilitate a healthy growth with progressive internalization and integration of each previous experience. One could observe transferences being similarly split into good and bad in Groups 1 and 2, though to a lesser extent than in Group 3. The best examples were offered by Mr Gage in Group 1. In retrospect his personality structure has to be diagnosed as a case of 'borderline personality organization'.

While in Group 1 there was only one participant with transference-split, all participants of Group 3 may be so described. Nevertheless, there were phases also in this group when participants managed to get away completely from this primitive transference level as if it did not exist. This denial occurred mostly when political themes dominated the group. These political questions were treated, especially by Marian and John, in a highly intellectual, abstract and theoretical fashion. Concealed behind such discussions were powerful destructive forces that could burst out without warning. On the other hand, I do not share the view, represented by Otto F. Kernberg,[3] that such processes appear in all groups and I certainly do not think that they appear in all small groups with ten or less participants. Large groups are a different matter. Their size is so threatening for the individual that even when a large group is composed of relatively healthy personalities, it splits into forces which are exclusively good and idealized and forces which are exclusively bad and destructive.[4] When such processes occur in small groups then, in my opinion, it is an indication that there are at least elements of borderline personalities among participants.

Borderline personality disorders stem from deprivations very early in the child's development. All participants of Group 3 had suffered such deprivations. Lucy, single and a manual worker, was born in 1946. Her parents, who worked in agriculture and were poor, left her on her own as a child. She experienced herself as being superfluous and sought compensation in pathologically intensified feeding, a case of 'extreme eating addiction', as she put it. Marian was born in 1947, a child unwanted by her parents, and grew up with the grandmother and an aunt. She had poor interpersonal relationships and suffered from ulcerative colitis, a psychosomatic illness coupled with ulcerated colon. Elsbeth, born in 1941, lost her father when she was three years old and among other things she had to replace the missing husband in her mother's life. Wilfrid, born in 1944, had a father, but grew up without having any relationship with him. He was pampered by his mother and, similarly to Elsbeth, he had to compensate for mother's deprivations. Eric, born in the same year, grew up in a marriage which was disturbed from the start. He did not have the necessary guidance from his father, and he too acted as a substitute for a frustrated mother. Grace, also born in 1944, without doubt had suffered the most severe damage of all. She never knew her father. Because of economic circumstances, her mother was often compelled to leave her on her own as a child. Moreover, the other participants, namely John, born in 1943, Evelyn, born in 1942 and Bill, born in 1939, whose families were all affected by the war, had suffered grave deprivations. Nevertheless, because of more fortunate social circumstances, contacts with other people somehow enabled these participants to compensate for the lack of parental care. Despite certain individual differences, the early deprivation of maternal care was common to all participants of this group. Naturally, this lack of care was largely due to the years of war during which most fathers were away. They were not there to comply with their function to protect the mothers and to be models for their children, as Hermann Roskamp pointed out in an article on identity conflicts of students born in the Second World War.[5] From a diagnostic point of view, all participants of Group 3 have to be classified in the first and second form of the so-called post-classical neuroses. To a large extent these forms coincide with the serious personality disorders described by Otto F. Kernberg.[6] Hence it is not surprising that this group developed a structure which corresponds exactly to what, in clinical psychology, is called borderline personality, as described above.

Chapter 11

Self-destruction of a group or the result of constructive separations?

1 Anarchy and chaos in Group 3

As Groups 1 and 2, so Group 3 also developed from the participants' life histories which they brought into the group through their contributions. A specific group process of its own evolved that I will sketch first in broad outline. Subsequently I will comment on it, pointing out its characteristic aspects.

The second session, in which all participants were present, started with Lucy reporting on her compulsive eating in her scarcely comprehensible dialect. With this contribution she struck the fundamental tone that persisted during the entire process and could never be ignored. The theme provoked great anxieties and, as in the first session, was defended against with sex talk of an aggressive sort. This was the 'oral' theme with insatiable wishes to get something which, at the same time, was experienced as something bad and repulsive. It was similar to what Mary experienced in Group 2. Despite her 'oral' disorder, Mary was able, however, to produce relatively mature ego-achievements, while this was not the case with Lucy. Outside the area of her work, Lucy was unable to make anything constructive of her relationships, especially the relationship with her partner. The same applies to most of the other participants of Group 3 as well, although some of them were professionally active, like Bill and Elsbeth, or in training like Evelyn and Grace. So it is little wonder that the group process was characterized by the participants' persistent unrelatedness among themselves as well as towards me as a conductor. For long stretches the picture presented by the group was chaotic. At the end of the second session in describing a dream, Evelyn managed to express how the individual members experienced the group: 'I dreamed of a large group. At first it was like being in a class at school. Everyone talked and wanted to be the speaker. After that a wild fight broke out.

In the end the idea was that all should urinate into a big pot.' This dream is commented upon by Marian, the Marxist girl, who says : 'Here we deal with such intimate matters.' After that all that remained for me to say was 'And that is frightening.'

2 'I am afraid of every person!'

The group tried to find its bearings in the midst of chaos. First, the participants hoped I would help them in their search for a direction. They talked about my role in the group and they looked for support, security and guidance from me. Then they began to look for help from each other. This hope gained expression when they started to use among themselves the familiar form of address – the German 'Du'. All the same they did not manage to conjure away the destructiveness. Without any regard for sensitivities, members were questioned about intimate details of their sex life. Thus the direction set by Elsbeth in the first session was found again and followed. A member had no feeling for the vulnerability of the other while he himself, or she herself, was most easily hurt. For instance, in the fourth session Marian, who was very destructive and insulting to others most of the time, had tears in her eyes, but was so ashamed because of it that she left the room abruptly. A group member dreamed that 'We all wear blue workers' uniform and heavy rucksacks. It is hard.' The participants' symptomatic relapses showed to what extent they suffered through their own aggressive attacks. Marian again had colitis, Bill's concentration was disturbed, John was no longer able to think and was afraid of losing his memory. Elsbeth went to see her physician because of other complaints and was absent over the following sessions. The voracious Lucy remained away from the group for several sessions.

The rest of the group talked about disappointed love, lack of trust towards women and fear of men. Grace touched upon the core of the problem when she said: 'I am not with you, I have not yet reached that point. I am afraid of every person.' For a while the group established a good relationship with Grace and genuinely tried to understand her. This atmosphere was again brutally destroyed by politicizing Marian when she returned to the group. She had sold her soul to her political activity and worked in a political group that rejected psychoanalysis. By accepting psychoanalytic group therapy, she put herself into a situation of conflict, of having to integrate in herself two opposites which were practically irreconcilable. She solved this problem conflict by splitting herself into two parts, neither of which knew the other one. The other participants lived with similar contradictions which they continually displayed in the group. They came to the session as to the place of safety which they dreaded at the same time. Each time the split-off, destructive parts prevented the establishment of good relationships and mutual understanding. When someone brought in a problem, then all the others felt that he was too demanding because everyone had another equally pressing problem. This happened to Erwin who had spent years in a sanatorium with tuberculosis. He brought the problem of being exploited by his girl-friends. After having slept with a girl, he becomes scared that she might get pregnant. Moreover, he is afraid of losing his flat and does not know how to carry on living without money. I say: 'Everyone has a serious problem. If he expresses it here, at first the burden becomes heavier for all, like in the dream with the rucksack. On the other hand, if we tried to carry it together, it would become progressively lighter.' Wilfrid doubts whether words can help. Eric feels he is oppressed by the women in the group. He wants to lean on the men, but then he is afraid of homosexuality. Elsbeth, expressing her current dilemma of whether to divorce or not, talks of the fear of bonds, something which, like a common group fantasy, applies more or less to everyone. This fear is apparent in the general mistrust in the group stemming from the fact that all the men had had very bad experiences with women as had all the women with men. I say: 'No one trusts anyone else, so bad were their previous experiences.' This statement is confirmed by Elsbeth. She recalls a scene when even her physician suddenly wanted to kiss her instead of concerning himself with her health. Following my interpretation, the group is afraid I would behave just like that. In the tenth session Bill tells of an experience from his childhood. When the French marched in, he, then six years old, saw how a party of soldiers set out to rape a group of women. The soldiers were so excited that they put down their weapons without taking notice of the child standing by. Bill wanted to grab the sub-machine gun next to him and shoot the men, but he was paralysed with great fear and could not do it. The group reacts to this account with alarm. In the next session Marian is absent and others arrive late. Grace feels she is excluded. Eric dreams of a car with, as he puts it, 'a brutally wide radiator'. He remembers his father who ignominiously left him in the lurch. All of a sudden, Wilfrid recalls that he never had contact with his father. When he once wanted to talk with him about this lack of contact, father wept and turned away. I say that the individual members are experiencing in the here and now the

lack of contact and therefore they have a chance this time to understand why it all happened in the first place. This interpretation
fails to bring relief or even peace. Some participants stay away and
others come late. Eventually, in the thirteenth session the core of the
group – without Marian, Lucy and Wilfrid – is close together, bound
through feelings of warmth and containment. These feelings in their
turn arouse anxiety and lead to the following associations. It is as if I
were 'taken', as if I were no longer myself; as if I did not exist for myself any more, but solely for others. Elsbeth remembers how her
mother used to question her about everything and how badly she spoke
about men. John recalls suddenly that his parents too used to do
nothing but question him all the time. Gudrun thinks that 'In the end
everything is held against one.' Only Bill retorts that it is not all that
bad, after all there are still chances of getting some help.

3 Testing to destruction

In the fifteenth session I have to tell the group that I have been invited
unexpectedly to go to the United States for the autumn. This means
that in addition to the summer holidays – on which we had agreed
when the group started – the sessions will unfortunately have to be
cancelled for a further four weeks. The group's reaction was: 'How are
we supposed to cope with that?'. Moreover, the group was intensely
preoccupied with the measures just taken   by the Federal German
Government. As at that time the mass of the students sympathized with
the Baader-Meinhof terrorist group, the police was empowered to search
flats and houses where university students lived. Some of the participants of Group 3 were professed sympathizers of the Baader-Meinhof
group. A fearful-delusional mood begins to spread. One is scared there
might be a tape recorder in the room; house searches might be impending; and there might be spies within the group. I interpret this mistrust as a result of disappointments. Participants had expected a lot
from me and now – at a time when the group had not yet completely
established itself – I announce that I will leave them out on a limb.
This interpretation was well understood, and had the effect of calming
the group down, thus leading to a phase of constructive co-operation.
Now Marian was able to report that her relationship with her boy-
friend had improved after he had separated from the other man who
was exploiting him. Elsbeth managed to present her petition for divorce.
Wilfrid found himself a better flat. Eric's fear that his girl-friend could

be pregnant turned out to be unfounded. Thereafter, he managed to start giving private music lessons, thus earning some money to resume his studies at the Academy of Music.

All of a sudden, in the midst of this constructive phase – which did not last long – destructive impulses broke through again. Nothing had helped, everything is shit (Marian), a clear line is missing (Elsbeth), all that is said is nothing but 'hypocrisy' (Grace). I remarked that though much of these sentiments might be justified, we have seen that there were also positive forces in the group. The latter had already brought about some improvements despite destructive tendencies. I could see that the group still felt very threatened, not least in view of the interruption of its work that I had announced. I finished by suggesting that we should talk about it in order to try to come to terms with rage. After that Marian is able to say that she does not feel at home anywhere. She becomes especially aggressive when she has a desire for tenderness, but her parents never understood that, nor did her grandmother. Yet she never ceased longing for someone who would understand it. Once she told her personal fate to a female teacher, whom she loved very much, by writing it down in a composition. The teacher, however, failed to understand the message altogether and dealt only with the formal errors in her composition. In that moment Marian had lost faith in humanity and felt herself worthless. In the nineteenth session Elsbeth cries thinking of her boy-friend of whom she is very fond, but who prefers other women to her. In the last session before summer holidays, she offers pumpkin seeds all around. Participants are eating the seeds while the talk whirls round confusion, catastrophe (Elsbeth), cold sweats (John), 'failure' (Wilfrid) and 'sanctimoniousness' (Grace).

During the holidays participants met in sub-groups. After that the group resumes its work with only four participants: Elsbeth, John, Eric and Bill. John reports a dream in which he was castrated by a physician and Eric talks about his mother who oppresses him. All participants become depressed and start talking about the anxiety caused by dependence and the desire to be dependent which is concealed behind that anxiety. After this interpretation the situation is clear and the tense atmosphere becomes relaxed. Then, two weeks after the end of the holiday break, Marian, Evelyn and Grace come back. The further process was characterized by the constantly simultaneous appearance of positive aspects – hope, trust and containment – and of destructive forces that broke through again and again. For instance, in the twenty-fourth session Grace says: 'I trust now, it helps!'. In the same session Marian says that nothing helped. Once more, despite the four weeks separation, all participants, except Lucy, are together again as previously. The difference is that now sub-groups have been formed who fight each other. Eric and Bill stick together as do Evelyn and Marian. This couple formation is supposed to protect against destructiveness which is now experienced even more intensely than before the break. A dream of Bill's shows how the group feels: 'A cow is led to the slaughter-house. It is a heifer, a young cow. She has a knife in her head.' Marian sees in me the group's murderer. She also states that she is pregnant, but under no circumstances would she like to have the child because 'parents should not have any children if they are unable to bring them up.' Like Bill in his dream, with this statement Marian expresses unequivocally to what extent the group feels not only abandoned by me, but outright ill-treated. In view of the actually oncoming interruption of the group process, I interpret this situation as a particularly drastic new version of past deprivations and ill-treatments. Later on there is a concerted attack against Marian while she denounced the lack of effective help and wears herself out in her political work. Bill feels the group is a circle 'with a hole in the middle into which one can fall at any time'. Memories of childhood deprivations are triggered off here and there through the difficulty of the real situation. Deprivations in the home of foster parents; deprivations because of absent fathers and fathers who were too weak and were dominated by mothers; deprivations because of inept mothers who in their turn had not received any maternal love. After the thirty-eighth session Elsbeth drops out without giving any notice. Already following the thirty-second session, Lucy failed to appear any more. The group members who were still present felt like bereaved relatives.

After overcoming the pain of separation and the bereavement, the group recovered for a while. In this constructive phase, it solved some problems in mutual co-operation. Having found a new and more satisfactory relationship, Eric separated from his previous girl-friend. He also found a better flat and became productive in his studies. Evelyn passed her exam successfully. John realized that his work as a clerk was only a poor temporary solution against which he unconsciously rebelled with his memory disorder. He now embarked on a new career. As after the forty-second session Wilfrid also was going to leave the group, I introduce – in agreement with the remaining participants – a new member in the forty-third session. She is Ursel, a 20-year-old student with learning difficulties and a speech disorder. She grew up in the countryside as the second of eight children. At present she is attached in a symbiotic, i.e. in a nearly 'melting' fashion, to her boy-friend who is going through a period of drug addiction. During her first session she silently observes the group and in the next session she describes it in this way: 'No one listens to the other. There is more talk about people outside than in the group. The contents revolve more round politics than feelings. What Mr Kutter says is either not heard or is torn to pieces.' In this way Ursel has held a mirror up in front of the group which was followed by a perplexed silence. In a later session Eric is able to speak, in a very empathetic way, about how pointlessly they all had thwarted each other and how much they had spoilt, although in reality each of them needed the other more than ever. Starting with the forty-fifth session, three further members drop out, namely Lucy, Elsbeth and Wilfrid. Thereafter, another new member joins the group: Maureen, a 26-year-old art student, exceptionally sophisticated and seductive in her appearance. She comes from an upper-middle-class family. As she had already had several psychoanalytic treatments, which she broke off, and countless interviews with psychotherapists, she is well versed in psychology. Her first contribution is a dream: 'The group is flying. It is threatened by friends. I have to say this to the conductor who obviously does not see the danger. At the end of the dream I am lying on a table, with spits stuck in my body.'

The group is deeply disconcerted by this evaluation on the part of a newcomer. John makes a forceful and yet disciplined effort to get the group out of its perplexity, but he has no followers. Eric reports another dream about the group: 'Everyone sits conspicuously separated from the other, the conductor even more aside, reading a book.' Eric adds his interpretation to this dream: 'Everyone is his own egoist.' We all understand the individuals' separation expressed in the dream not as a progress towards individuation, but as a loss. This meaning is confirmed by the fact that the participants pull closer together, the heads leaning forward. They seem to have only one common thought, namely to protect the group against its disintegration.

4 A group's agony

The subsequent process leaves no room for doubt about the group's progressive disintegration. Ursel and Maureen attack each other, with mutual reproaches for intellectualizing, lacking femininity and understanding. During the further course of events Maureen does what she unconsciously had announced in her dream: after a suicide attempt, with admission to hospital, she compels me to give her individual interviews. During these interviews she runs down the group. Then, conversely, in the group sessions, she evaluates the group positively and voices her low opinion of me as a therapist who is no better than all the others, who has no interest in his patients and who behaves in a plainly irresponsible fashion. In this way she splits the group. At the same time she describes how she has been exploited by men whom she trusted so that in the end she could only weep when they had sexual intercourse with her. Around this time John also leaves the group after having expressed his anxiety about the murderously raging women (Ursel, Maureen and Evelyn). He closes ranks with his girlfriend and looks − as she has done − for individual therapy. A few sessions later Grace also drops out. She too tries to get individual therapy.

The remnants of the group − compared with the beginning just a torso − stay together for about another six months. Now massive destructive forces appear and, more than ever before, Maureen's bad dream comes true. She mercilessly runs down the therapist and the group while outside she begins to establish a good relationship with another therapist. In a dream Ursel kills her rival and because of that she goes to jail. Other dreams are about illness and death (Bill, Ursel and Maureen in the fifty-seventh session). Memories revolve round how parents mutually tear each other to pieces (Eric), the parents' negligence, indifference and coldness. After these feelings had been interpreted in relation to the therapist, cold mothers and irresponsible fathers surface from the depths. At last in the sixty-seventh session Maureen deals the death-blow to the group by calling it a 'shit group' and praising another group at the same time. She labels the therapist dogmatic and repressive as all therapists are. They all sit on the longer end of the lever, recklessly using their power, without the slightest personal interest in their patients' progress, but her new therapist treats her free of charge. Although he does not belong to any psychoanalytic school, he is the first one who understands her. More dreams follow: a concentration camp with emaciated people who are supervised (seventieth session); a fly sitting in the vagina and sucking out the contents of the abdomen (seventy-second session); a cat with its throat cut through (seventy-third session); and breasts at which a gigantic mouth sucks (seventy-fifth session). The associations are about weak fathers who are kept under mother's thumb, complete failures who are unable to protect the children from 'devouring' mothers (seventy-ninth session). The participants feel like unwanted children, deserted by the mothers or not ever accepted. This feeling is clearest in the case of Bill who spent the first two years of his life with his grandparents. After a further two years with foster parents, the mother at last accepted him when he was four years old. With his father he could not have any relationship at all.

The remainder of the group dissolved after the ninety-eighth session. In that last session the participants declared that despite all the destruction and sadness caused by the ending of the group, on the whole they were now better off than when they started.

5   Theoretical retrospect

If we examine the steps of this process in the light of our model, it will be easy to place Group 3 in sub-layers IIb and IIc. The participants suffer not only from narcissistic personality disorders, but they also show symptoms of the so-called borderline personality organization,[1] i.e. symptoms of the borderline syndrome. They are regressed to the oral stage of drive organization (Lucy with her voracious food 'addiction'), are unable to deal with their emotions in a constructive manner and from the beginning project unintegrated, split-off, destructive forces on to the group. They hit others without being able to see how they do it. There is no mutual empathy. One ruthlessly penetrates the others by questioning them about their sex problems. The lack of impulse control indicates ego-weakness which is stated directly by Gudrun when she says: 'I am not with you, I have not yet reached that point.' It is also expressed in Bill's dream: the rucksack is too heavy. Drive eruptions, unsolved attachments with the tendency of wanting to cling to, to oppress and to swallow the other person, are illustrated by the example of Elsbeth's mother. These tendencies become particularly clear in the dream about the fly in the vagina which sucks up the contents of the abdomen. Although the group is frightened by all this, for long stretches it is unable to free itself from these oppressing and parasitical objects which are experienced as being the conductor and the other participants. The group is seen as a perilous hole into which one might fall. The conductor is looked upon as weak, disappointing, unreliable and irresponsible. This feeling has an element of reality as the long break — which stretched over several weeks during the first year of treatment — unavoidably provoked a strong impression of being deserted.

As they were robbed of protection by an authority, the participants, who have not yet become sufficiently independent, could not do anything but experience each other as mutually exploiting objects. In retrospect, it was quite sensible for participants to protect themselves from the exploiting attacks of others by leaving the group so that they got rid of the damaging object. It was not mere coincidence that the participants who had dropped out managed to develop relatively well afterwards outside the group which they had experienced as very threatening. Wilfrid found a new flat; John started to study for a new career; Grace sought individual therapy; Elsbeth worked and found a new boy-friend who understood her better than her ex-husband; Marian freed herself from the clutches of her political group and began to devote herself more to her studies. These good relationships could only be established because the bad and damaging ones were left behind in the group. Therefore, it was rather difficult for the remnant group to get rid of its destructive forces or to transform them into constructive ones. Here the good relationships were continually threatened with destruction like the women were threatened by the raping soldiers as the six-year-old Bill saw them — and as the soldiers were threatened by the possibility that Bill might shoot them down with the submachine gun. Trust was continually followed by mistrust: microphones in the room, the idea of spies and house-searching. At times it seemed as if the positive and shielding forces could keep in check the destructive negative ones, but this hope turned out to be only a big illusion. The existential threat persisted: the cow with the knife in the head, the cat with the cut throat, the concerted attack against Marian, the danger the conductor fails to see and Maureen lying on the table with spits stuck in her body. Without the work of Melanie Klein,[2] it would be difficult to understand these elemental destructive forces. They have become even clearer through the more recent work of Otto F. Kernberg[3] mentioned earlier (Chapter 10.4). The rage of wanting to destroy everything becomes comprehensible because of the envy directed against the conductor: his unfair advantages due to his knowledge, his power, his house. It is an envy which corresponds to the envy of the infant — let us recall the dream with the breasts and the gigantic mouth —

the infant who has been abandoned by the mother and who screams and is not heard. Despite these destructive instinctual impulses, the prevalent primitive defence mechanisms, the splitting into good and bad and the objects experienced as swallowing one or sucking one out — like the fly in the vagina, or objects that one swallows — breasts and mouth, despite all this, individual participants should have been able to recognize that not everything is doomed. They should have known that Mephisto is wrong when he says:[4]

> The spirit I, that endlessly denies.
> And rightly, too; for all that comes to birth
> Is fit for overthrow, as nothing worth;
> Wherefore the world were better sterilized.

In retrospect one can see that notwithstanding its great destructive potential, little by little the group did succeed in unburdening itself of these negative forces. By realizing that it could not destroy the conductor, the group experienced something indestructible, something that seemingly is capable of withstanding all attacks and destruction. The conductor's survival proves that the split-off, bad parts after all are not as devastating as one feared they would be. Following this path, in the end it was possible to recognize one's own bad parts as such and to integrate them into a more mature pattern. The result was a more stabilized identity. The ego was now strong enough to separate itself from a restrictive, oppressive and destructive object and so become free.

Chapter 12

Sexuality and the Oedipus complex in the group

1 Men help women to become women and women help men to become men

In the first session of the students' group when Elsbeth spoke openly about her inability to experience orgasm and asked the other women whether they had orgasm, the sex theme was merely used as a defence against anxiety. Behind the sex theme there was a great fear of impulses which were not integrated, but split off and mostly aggressively cathected. In fact, these impulses did appear in the further course of the group process. It was different in Group 1 where each participant — except the dynamic Mr Gage — has relived the various developmental stages of infantile sexuality. Mrs Murphy displaced her transference love from the conductor to Mr Morgan. The latter in his turn developed an affection towards Mrs Sinfield which was the reproduction of his love towards his own sister. Later on Mr Morgan managed to channel this emotion towards Mrs Murphy. This was a kind of love which did not really belong to the other person, but to a transference object. From a psychoanalytical point of view, one can say that this love sprang from a repetition compulsion.

It was not always easy to work through sexuality in this group. Masculine stirrings among men triggered off desires for masculinity among women as well. Over long stretches these desires were so strong that the men stood in fear of losing their masculinity. In this way the women also managed to defend themselves against the anxiety of being in a feminine position *vis-à-vis* the men, for they unconsciously feared submission and injury. In the process of working through sexual conflicts, the following phases could be distinguished: In a first phase, the women rejected the ungovernable sexuality of the men who consequently felt castrated by the women. At the same time the women felt raped by the men. In a second phase the men were able to renounce

their phallic sexuality — which was pressing them for impulse gratification — and to tolerate the women's need for love. At the same time the
men recognized the aggressive parts of their phallic sex desires which
originated in the anal-sadistic and oral-sadistic stages. Gradually the
women were also able to work through their own sadistic parts in their
dealings with men. The main motivation for their sadistic attitudes
was the desire for revenge, for earlier disillusionments with significant
male objects, on the men in the group. In a third phase the women
managed to tolerate the men's position and to become more and more
feminine. In this phase the men, having overcome the fear of being
castrated, could behave in a more masculine fashion. Finally, in a
fourth phase the men's task was to incorporate feminine desires in
themselves, while the women had to achieve a better integration of
strong masculine parts into their personality. This integration was
possible only after the third phase during which participants had
learned to feel strong and secure enough in the position of their own
sex. It was also helpful that through new significant persons a mature,
non-neurotic sexuality streamed from outside into the group. Mrs
Murphy met a native Bavarian, an uninhibited son of nature, whom
she surnamed the 'woodcutter'. Mrs Faulkner had frequent encounters
with a passionate Jugoslav. Obviously these men — more than the men
in the group or the conductor — knew how to help the female participants to learn to experience themselves as women. Moreover, these
men outside the group indirectly helped the male participants too.
The latter, through an unconscious homosexual identification with
the 'woodcutter' and the Jugoslav, could strengthen their own masculine position.

To sum up, the female participants' relationships with other men
outside the group not only directly helped the women to deal with
their disturbed sexual development but, through identification, these
relationships also helped the men. Both enriched the group process and
forcefully propelled it forward. Now sexual partnership became
possible in the sense of mature genitality. The partner was no longer
seen only as the object of drive gratification or the occasion for satisfying desires for revenge. The partner was now experienced as another
person who in his (her) turn has his (her) own needs. Instead of dis-
puting each other's needs, thanks to 'cross-identifications' men and
women could now even feel each other's needs in an empathetic fashion.

2 The precondition of mature sexual relations: overcoming the Oedipus complex

A typically different configuration emerged in Group 2. Basically all participants suffered similar disturbances in their sexual development to the participants of Group 1. The roots of those disturbances were, however, not only religious and moral taboos internalized at an early age. The sexual disturbances in Group 2 originated from incestuous bonds to the parent of the opposite sex. Participants regressed to the anal-sadistic position of infantile sexual development driving the group into sado-masochistic relationships, with participants tormenting each other. This was the case especially between Ralph and Mary. Like a married couple who mutually oppress each other, they prevented each other from developing further. Behind all this, and thriving on a deeper level, there was the hidden fear of being abandoned. To varying extents, this anxiety was shared by all participants. Apart from the elements belonging to the anal-sadistic stage, the infantile sexuality of this group had a prevalently oral character. This means that the participants – like one- to two-year-old children – sought the exclusive attention of the conductor. In later stages of development of Group 3 the transferences to the conductor clearly corresponded to incestuous relationships between daughter and father (Mary), mother and son (Ralph). Since the therapeutic situation does not allow the gratification of such wishes, unavoidably these transferences led to frustration followed by corresponding rage. This rage was directed against the frustrating object whom one wanted to destroy. Nevertheless, the rage in this group did not reach the same proportions as in Group 3.

The participants' partners were relieved of undue pressures to the same extent to which the group members managed to transfer on to the conductor their sexual desires and fears as well as their reactions to the rejection of these desires. Gisela – who had already had a hundred sessions of group therapy before joining Group 2 – now fell in love with the conductor in the same way as she had been in love with her father when she was a small girl. Louise expected unlimited attention and Mary unconsciously wanted to have a child by the conductor.

All three forms of behaviour were a revival of the positive Oedipal configuration in which the daughter loves the father and hates the mother. The participants, however, were now able to become aware of these feelings, especially of the rage caused by rejection. The fact that the conductor – unlike individual group members before – did not unconsciously identify himself with this rejecting role, enabled the group to bring these feelings to a more conscious level, thus overcoming them in favour of a mature sexuality. Once these conflicts were resolved through the person of the conductor, the participants could experience the other person not as a transference object, but as a real person.

3 The Oedipus complex re-enacted in the here and now

The Oedipal situation in the mother-father-child triangle constitutes the central problem of neurosis. As it also plays an important role in groups, we want to look at it more closely. From the early phases of the group process the triadic configuration of the Oedipus complex can be reflected in transference and counter-transference between conductor and participants. Subsequently, however, it serves mostly as a defence against sibling rivalry or against pre-Oedipal conflicts, i.e. conflicts predating the triadic Oedipal configuration. It is only much later − when the group as a whole is further regressed and relives the infantile scene − that the conflict is experienced directly in its full power, more or less involving everyone. It has to be noted that the positive form of the Oedipus complex often serves as resistance against its reverse, namely the negative Oedipus complex. The positive form consists in the son loving the mother and hating the father, while the daughter loves the father and hates the mother. Conversely, we speak of the negative Oedipus complex when the son loves the father and hates the mother, while the daughter loves the mother and hates the father. The following example taken from the 149th session of Group 1 is a typical illustration of the positive Oedipus complex. The dynamic Mr Gage starts the session by complaining of difficulties at work and of a dazed feeling in his head. He directs his complaints mostly at Mrs Sheen who sits next to him to the right. It is plain that love towards Mrs Sheen is at work in this interaction and that it is the son's love towards the mother. Our nice factory-girl, however, does not react to the young man's advances. Instead she once more grumbles about her husband who comes home too late and continually pesters her with sex. As Mr Gage intensifies his advances, Mr Pittman cuts him short and starts to speak about his own professional ambitions, and how he feels constrained by bosses and colleagues. At this point I interpret the struggle between the two men as rivalry for Mrs Sheen's attention. Thereupon Mrs Faulkner joins in, and, while leaning towards me, talks about her unhappy love for her partner. She had already conveniently chosen to sit next to me, on my left. Meanwhile there was the love affair between Mr Morgan and Mrs Sinfield, known to everyone because of the disclosure about their Sunday outing. Mr Gage was jealous of this relationship, while Mrs Murphy showed clear signs of jealousy because of Mrs Faulkner's advances towards the conductor.

Summing up, there were at least four kinds of triadic configurations in this session:

1 between Mr Gage, Mr Pittman and Mrs Sheen. In a positive Oedipal configuration both men experienced Mrs Sheen as the rejecting mother, while I represented the much hated father;

2 between Mrs Faulkner, Mrs Murphy and myself. In a positive Oedipal configuration, Mrs Faulkner experienced in me the beloved and unresponsive father, and Mrs Murphy saw in me the hated mother;

3 between Mr Morgan, Mrs Sinfield and Mr Gage as the excluded third party;

4 also between Mrs Murphy, myself and Mrs Faulkner. The latter was experienced by Mrs Murphy as the unconsciously dreaded mother.

This mesh of classical triadic Oedipal relationships served also as resistance against other desires concealed behind it. These desires were those corresponding to the negative Oedipus complex as well as desires for an unrestrained dyadic relationship with the conductor. However, it took months before the group could see the passive desires, shared by all, for being accepted, loved and admired. These were the desires embedded in the triadic conflicts in which one was always excluded and which were fraught with jealousies. Therefore, the triadic relationships described also had a defensive character, although not to the same extent by far as in Group 2.

4 Homosexuality in the group

In the further course of the group process, the men in Group 1 represented by Mr Gage as their speaker, increasingly developed sexual desires directed towards the conductor. A dream gave advance notice of this development: 'I am fighting vigorously with a powerful man. In the end an embrace evolves out of the fight. I wake up full of anxiety.'

The group's associations to this dream showed that the male participants did not wish to rival each other or the conductor at all. What they really wanted was to be loved by the conductor. Their desire, however, which corresponded to the negative Oedipus complex, was fearfully avoided for two main reasons: one, such desires were felt to be homosexual in character and therefore forbidden; two, they were frightening desires because of traumatic experiences in childhood. In the case of Mr Gage these passive homosexual desires broke through with such a force that, due to his unstable personality structure, he fell into panic and anxiety, became very disturbed and had to leave the group for several weeks. The homosexual impulses that were awakened were so strong as to threaten to overwhelm his weak ego. The other men managed more and more to admit their positive relationships to the conductor and among themselves. They achieved this by working through feelings of shame and guilt *vis-à-vis* the women as well as through the threat immediately feared in the homosexual relation. Thus, these relationships became fruitful for the group process. In a later phase the positive Oedipal configuration could be cathected again in a direct form and be worked through further. Thus, the course of this group's development conformed to a large extent to the principles I have described elsewhere.[1]

5 Escape into dependence or fight for independence?

In Group 2 it was far more difficult to work through infantile sexuality. Again and again oral fixations delayed working through Oedipal conflicts. The group experienced the conductor as being very rejecting orally, as a cruel object that lets one go hungry. Mary's unconscious wish was that the conductor at last would give her something so that she could be cured from her vomiting. It should be something so good that she does not have to spit out again and again what she has eaten. In the same way, the conductor should help Ralph to gain greater male potency. Everyone has the wish to get something concrete which, if they can get it, will free them from their symptoms. The group sought an exclusively dyadic relationship with the conductor. Later on this became a triadic relationship in that Group 2 created an inter-group conflict. It felt intensely jealous of Group 1 thinking that the latter was better cared for by me. At the end of a session this jealousy reached such a point that some participants decided to remain seated. They wanted to force a confrontation with the other group, which they envied, and at the same time they were punishing the conductor for his inadequacy. In the further course of the group process such acting out could be interpreted as fear of masculine behaviour among the men and fear of the feminine position among women. These anxieties arose because the group members did not yet feel strong enough.

The participants avoided sexual behaviour in relation to the opposite sex. Instead, they fell back again and again into the attitude of oral expectation. The men tried to receive orally that 'indefinable something', namely the analyst's masculine potency. The women imagined in their unconscious fantasy a proto-feminine woman who could secure for them all they still lacked to become potent in a healthy feminine way. After a progressive move towards their own autonomous potentials, the participants succeeded little by little in overcoming these desires. The 40-year-old vicar George, a participant of Group 2 whom we have not yet mentioned, made a decisive contribution towards this change. In the 111th session, on his own initiative he brought bread, distributed it among the participants, thus supplying them symbolically, as in the Lord's Supper, with what they were longing for. Later on participants could identify themselves with admired models of the same sex. These identifications helped them to gain stability in their own sex identity. Thereafter, participants were able to free themselves from their fixation on the dyadic relationship and from their passive desires for specific nourishment from the conductor. As in Group 1, here also Oedipal triadic configurations were the next step. Participants were afraid that the father, experienced as the conductor, would turn away from them and direct his attention to mother. In the 121st session this primal scene became very real and was relived in the here and now. In this scene the child covets the parent of the opposite sex and it has to experience most painfully that the parent does not turn to him, but to the other parent of the same sex. The child experiences this move as its hurtful exclusion. This scene was enacted in the group as follows. Without any apparent reason Mary gets excited. She blushes and can hardly stand staying with the group. Ralph speaks of an indefinable anxiety. Albert feels not only anxious, but completely deserted. George shivers with cold without being able to say why. I interpret the situation by saying that Mary and I are seen by the others as a couple. The rest of the group is jealous and feels excluded. Mary suddenly remembers a dream in which she had experienced sexual excitement towards her father. As she completely rejects him on a conscious level, it is hard for her even to imagine such an excitement. Now it became possible to acknowledge the fear of incest, to acknowledge the naturalness of such desires and the pertinent jealousy and to go on working through these feelings. An interim period followed in which participants of the same sex could identify with each other without too much fear of being taken for homosexuals. Then a phase of fierce rivalry ensued which was geared mainly to dispossess the conductor of his power. In the 146th session of Group 2 George, the vicar, sat on the chair that up to then was reserved for me. By doing so, he literally took over my place. The other men attacked me verbally. Also the women took part in the rivalrous arguments with me. In the transference they relived the hatred against their own fathers. Without letting me have my say, they stopped me altogether. This aggressive struggle naturally included the working through of guilt feelings related to the Oedipal triumph, namely the triumph over the father. The group came out of this struggle invigorated, with new initiatives and creative capacity.

The common themes of the phases described were sexuality and the Oedipus complex. These themes were experienced differently by each individual, in accordance with the point in the group process and the group member's position in this process. Each participant was entangled in a changing position within the triadic Oedipal conflict. Nevertheless, love and hatred between three people – with one of the three being excluded at any given time – was the conflict common to all participants. In this way it is possible to work through individuals' personal conflicts historically, as well as through group conflicts shared by all participants.

Chapter 13
Aggressiveness in the group

1 Various forms and kinds of aggressiveness

Aggressiveness can be considered as a second drive next to sexuality, or as a consequence of rejection or as both. Whether we adopt one or the other view, aggressiveness plays a decisive role in determining the course of events in the group. Its main thrust moves from the group towards the conductor. To this extent it can be understood and managed as in individual analysis. On the other hand, as it appears also between group members, aggression in the group and its management is at the same time specifically different from aggressiveness in individual analysis.

The analyst distinguishes a secondary aggressiveness as symptom — used to defend against anxiety or against sexual desires — and a primary aggressiveness which is not a defence. Both types can appear in different forms:

1   In mature, neutralized form as hatred felt by one person against another or against a group;
2   In less neutralized form, as so-called narcissistic rage;
3   In immature, primitive, un-neutralized form as destructiveness that wants to smash everything.

These three kinds of aggressiveness can be related easily to our three therapy groups. In Group 1 there was hatred directed against someone, but without a wish to destroy that person. This is the first form of aggressiveness listed above. In Group 2 the second form prevailed, namely a rage resulting from being hurt. Finally, Group 3 was characterized by an aggressiveness which is out to destroy. It revealed itself from the very beginning in the inconsiderate way in which participants questioned each other. As outlined in Chapter 11, the destructiveness escalated to violent attacks during the subsequent phases. There were different individual reactions to the general group destructiveness:

a worsening of Marian's ulcerative colitis, John's memory disorders, the depressions of the other participants. This aggressiveness was interpreted as a reaction to the fear of being hurt by others and to the fear that the conductor as well as the group might be destroyed. This interpretation created an aggression-free atmosphere in which individual participants were able to bring in their personal problems. Soon afterwards, however, the destructiveness flared up again.

Aggression might also indicate a progressive move towards reality. Here is an example from Group 2. The events occurred at a later phase of the process, namely in the 133rd session. Two sessions had been cancelled and the first one after this break starts with complaints about vomiting, headaches, anxiety and depressions. Given the point the group process had reached, it was easy to recognize that these symptoms were reactions to the break which was experienced as rejection. Several participants remembered how they were left in the lurch in their childhood. William recalled that his father had often been away. Gisela spoke about her father's illness, Mary painfully remembered having been tortured by her step-father and how, at the same time, he tried to seduce her. Given this situation it was obvious that a transference interpretation was called for: the group experienced the break as the members had earlier experienced being left in the lurch by their respective fathers. In the following sessions participants managed to get away from their symptoms and to express the pent up aggression, concealed behind the symptoms by taking the conductor to task: 'You did not help us. You did not give us anything. We are hurt because of this and we all have the right to feel hurt!' These expressions had a liberating effect and led to a further improvement in the symptoms.

2 Aggression in the family, narcissistic rage and primitive destructiveness

In Group 1 it was important to work through the aggressiveness which was concealed unconsciously in the attempted sexual advances. It became clear that the aggressive elements — which immediately prompted the other party to reject the erotic advances — were nothing but reactions to childhood disappointments which had been relived in the group. The deliberate courting by the men — for example Mr Morgan's courting of Mrs Sheen and Mrs Murphy — unconsciously contained elements of simple revenge. This was the same motive that induced the women to reject the men. Only after these revenge elements had been slowly dismantled and dropped on both sides, could a mature and co-operative partnership relation start and grow. This new spirit of co-operation enabled participants to organize and undertake a trip abroad together to Vienna.

While aggression between the group and the conductor corresponds to the child-parent relationship, the aggressive behaviour among participants often reflects sibling rivalry in the family. For instance, in the first session of Group 2 Ralph experienced, first unconsciously and then with growing awareness, the three female participants as his three elder sisters. In childhood, they had oppressed and restricted him, thus reinforcing the repression already exerted by his mother. In Group 1 Mr Morgan repeated his loving devotion to his sister in the love he felt towards Mrs Sinfield. In Group 3 Ursel experienced the group as a replica of her own family. She had exactly the same number of siblings as the number of participants in the group. In such cases the siblings' jealousy of father's or mother's love is predominant. The group has become the exact copy of the family.[1]

During the main phase of the process aggression in groups arises from the Oedipus complex. Impulses to murder and death wishes go hand in hand with it. Due to such impulses Mr Gage (Group 1) would dearly have loved to kill me many times. His hatred was so intense that the others reacted to it with alarm and feared to lose their conductor. In Group 2 Albert experienced these impulses first as compulsive thoughts against his own children. In the further course of the group process, however, he managed to transfer these impulses and direct them against me. Once they were interpreted, he managed to understand that these impulses were death wishes against his father. The latter had caused his severe foot injury on the bicycle. In a dream Mary killed her husband and the other participants also harboured death wishes. Naturally the mobilization of such forbidden sentiments leads to corresponding defence reactions, followed by a worsening of symptoms. Both have to be worked through in the transference to the conductor in the same way as in individual analysis. In the group, however, it is easier to work through aggressiveness. Everyone is in the same situation and can transfer death wishes on to one member while at the same time loving others.

Aggressiveness arising from the Oedipus complex dominated the main phases of Groups 1 and 2. In addition, in Group 2 the narcissistic rage (see Chapter 13.1) appeared as a consequence of the group's self-esteem being hurt. As the members of Group 3 constituted borderline cases between neurosis and psychosis, destructiveness (see Chapter 13.1) was the characteristic feature of their aggressive transactions and they were unable to find any mature ways of settling differences among themselves or with the conductor. Severe deprivations in early childhood, mostly in the relationship with the mother, had prevented participants from neutralizing and integrating the primitive preliminary stages of their aggressiveness into more constructive forms. A group composed of such participants needs something more in addition to an intensive and continuous analytic psychotherapy of the classical type. With such a group the analyst will have to behave in a particularly reliable, patient and steadfast manner. He has to be able to stand up to the destructive attacks of the group so as to give it the chance of 'working off' its destructive impulses on his person. For this purpose he has to create a specially reliable and permanently protective atmosphere. Such an environment has the double function of enabling the group to grow as well as of proving itself indestructible *vis-à-vis* the group's destructive impulses. As we have seen in the process of Group 3, this is a difficult task and the conductor is not always able to tackle it in the best possible way. Today I would not take such a group unless certain conditions are fulfilled. For instance, there should be no interruptions during the initial phase. The conductor should not be under great pressures but should be in a favourable position so as to fulfil what Winnicott calls the 'holding function'. In short, the conductor should be able to offer a facilitating environment which promotes the maturational process.[2]

Chapter 14

The conductor's function

1 The influence of the conductor's technique on the group process

Together with the participants the conductor creates the group's 'culture', its 'style', that is to say, the way each person deals with the other. In so far as he maintains this objective in view and decides on the method of proceeding, the conductor unquestionably exerts a leadership function. His ability to observe and understand as well as his interpretation technique have a decisive influence on the group process. In this sense a therapy group is of necessity conductor-centred. At the same time it is also participant-centred as the driving forces emanate from the individual participants, from the pressure of their suffering and their desire to progress. The conductor's task is essentially to keep on pinpointing the resistances all the time, and again and again, which stand in the way of these driving forces (see Chapter 6).

The group-as-a-whole possesses in itself a driving force which enables it to learn, to maintain itself in an 'optimal tension', without over-reaching itself, to register whenever this tension slackens and to correct the deviation by itself. To this extent the group being a self-regulating system is also constantly group-centred.

Having to conform to the group's composition, the conductor's behaviour and style of intervention are different from group to group. From the description of the three groups the reader will have seen how different the group process can be even when the conductor uses basically the same procedures. If the participants — as those in Group 1, for instance — are able to experience the conductor as a whole person, such as a mother or a father, then a so-called transference neurosis develops. In the conductor's person they relive all the experiences they had with significant objects of their early childhood and in the course of their subsequent development. These group members can be expected to cope with the usual analytic technique which requires the analyst to behave in a largely passive and abstinent fashion. The conductor comments only when he deems it necessary to help participants to recognize their own problems. In order to achieve the aim – which is to lead participants to solve their problems by themselves – the conductor facilitates a consistent working through of the conflicts in the transference field between himself and the group. To ever varying extents he is experienced as the dreaded castrating father or as the beloved father, as the seductive and/or rejecting mother. It is hoped that Chapters 7 and 13 were helpful in driving home the importance of working through these transferences which in the course of the process often change, being sometimes loaded with eroticism and sometimes charged with pronounced aggressiveness.

The conductor's analytic reserve is likely to put excessive stress on patients, as on those in Group 2, who suffer from narcissistic personality disorders in the sense described by Heinz Kohut.[1] This is especially so if the interpretations are directed exclusively to the group and disregard the individual altogether. Narcissistic patients can barely tolerate the analyst's neutral attitude and his group interpretations. In a group composed of such participants it is advisable to 'accept' as it were without hesitation the narcissistic idealizing transference in the sense Heinz Kohut describes it. This transference will give the group a chance to develop a healthy self-esteem. As a matter of principle the same applies, however, to all therapy groups. Problems of self-esteem have to be taken into account even with patients suffering from pure classical neuroses, though their self-esteem problems might be less serious than those of severely disturbed people – like those in Group 3. In Group 1 it was Mr Gage more than any one else who as 'speaker' of the group often managed to express and articulate very well the group's self-valuation – or one could even call it the 'group's self-esteem'. He was also the one who reacted like a seismograph to offences against the group-as-a-whole. In practice it is often difficult to uphold the principle of minimum structure.[2] This approach is hardly tolerated by groups whose participants suffer from narcissistic personality disorders – like those of Group 2, or who represent borderline cases with their characteristic 'transference split', as in Group 3. In my opinion it is not wrong at all to address individual participants during the initial phase of such groups, whenever they appear to be particularly restless or exhausted without yet being able to express themselves. To create a facilitating environment for such patients the conductor may also structure the sessions to a certain extent but, of course, without going too far in doing so. What is required is an 'optimum structure' rather than a 'minimum structure'. Without an optimum structure the participants would experience great anxieties, tend towards a kind of fragmentation of their personality with the danger of breaking down, followed by mounting defence and the worsening of symptoms. The group process as a whole would take an unsatisfactory course as was illustrated by the events in Group 3. Judging it in retrospect, a firmer structure would most probably have been more beneficial for the individuals as well as for the group-as-a-whole. With patients who, like the participants of the students' group, suffer from more or less severe disorders of the 'borderline personality organization' type, the methods used to cure drug addicts are more likely to lead to success. These methods include more frequent sessions, longer therapy, an unconventional style in a warm atmosphere emanating security and offering the opportunity to satisfy desires for attachment, tenderness and direction. A certain degree of real fulfilment of these needs creates the preconditions that later on enable participants to tolerate the psychoanalytic approach which is bound to provoke a higher degree of frustration.

Towards the end of the group process the conductor gradually loses his significance and becomes more and more dispensable. At times the group's potency becomes superior to that of the conductor. When such a phase is reached, the group often holds a mirror in front of the conductor. It is then that the group is really group-centred. We will return to this point when discussing the end phase in Chapter 16.

2 The influence of the group process on the conductor's technique

As already mentioned (see Chapter 9.1), irrespective of the conductor's attributes, his age, sex or technique, the group process evolves according to what the participants contribute to it. Among these contributions are the inevitable conflicts of the sexes in relation to each other, the problem of sexuality, that of aggression, the theme of the early mother-child relationship and, last but not least, the problem of authority. The latter surfaces very quickly, especially in the initial phase when the participants' fantasies still circle round the conductor as the pivotal figure. He is experienced as the rejecting mother and/or dreaded as the punishing father or vice versa. The whole struggle, which once was defended against, has to be replayed on his person. In the positive Oedipal position, this replay arouses the anxiety that one might be punished if one dares to take the conductor's place. In the negative Oedipal position the anxieties are about being considered unmanly, infantile or even effeminate if one asks something from the conductor, receives something from him. This theme was beautifully illustrated in the last session of the students" group before the summer break (see Chapter 11.3) when Elsbeth brought pumpkin kernels to eat during the session. By doing so she showed the group, and the conductor, how much she wanted him to give her nourishment and that such a desire was far from being satisfied. In addition, receiving nourishment can acquire a specific sexual meaning. One can, for instance, unconsciously experience the pumpkin kernels not only as if they were milk, but also as if they stood for sperm. Fantasies of receiving a child from the conductor also belong to this sphere of meaning. Among male participants violent homosexual anxieties might arise at first reinforcing the resistances. This was the case in Group 1 when, for a time, Mr Gage was caught up in an outright homosexual 'panic' with paranoid symptoms. This panic prompted him to run away from the group temporarily. Such a reaction, however, is unusual and was due to the particularly unstable ego-structure of this patient. He probably would have fitted in better in Group 2 where, through the idealizing transference of the initial phase, he could have built up the necessary self-confidence. This basis would have given him the strength to work through the Oedipal problem. His example teaches us how important it is to make sure that participants selected for a group are not too different in kind and seriousness of their ailments. Also group members' ages should not be too disparate. Groups that develop a transference neurosis towards the conductor and other participants – like Group 1 – create a different group process, through the individual participants' contributions, from that of groups with narcissistic transferences – like Group 2, and with splitting transferences – like Group 3. Accordingly, the conductor's technique has to be specifically different in each case.

3 The individual participant's influence

The conductor has to know the history of each individual participant and his individual dynamic. This is the prerequisite enabling him to make the problem of a participant the object of analysis during one or several sessions, without harm to the others. The conductor can do this by starting from a relevant point in the here and now and then letting the group work on the problem and thus test its own psychoanalytic potency. In Group 1 it was Mrs Sheen with her hysterical structure who largely dominated the initial phase of the group process. She brought into the group the so-called 'phallic' theme of the woman, i.e. the problem concerning the woman's masculine side. As explained in Chapter 6, in this connection one had constantly to consider the defence aspect as well. In Group 2 it was Mary with her obstinate vomiting symptom who managed again and again to call in question the conductor's and the group's potency. Unconsciously she brought into the group the mechanism of her symptom by accepting and, nearly through the same act, destroying the conductor's interpretations. In Group 3, the students' group, it was Marian who determined the entire initial phase of nearly forty sessions. Spell-bound by the ideology of her political group, and speaking in a highly intellectualizing fashion, she entered into a violent rivalry with the conductor. She often devalued him, thus seriously threatening the very existence of the already unstable group.

There are two ways in which individuals might determine the group process:

1 the individual acts as the speaker of the group and expresses what the group thinks;
2 the individual distances himself from the group process and introduces an individual problem.

Nevertheless, even the introduction of an individual problem expresses a group problem, namely the conflict between an individual and the rest of the group. Such a conflict is always of concern to the group-as-a-whole. To put it differently, individual and collective themes coincide.

4 The conductor's counter-transference

We mean by counter-transference the conductor's reactions to the group's transference as well as to the transference of individual participants. Counter-transference is an important instrument for understanding what is going on in the group and for understanding what the group, or the individual participant, so to speak, 'does to' the conductor. Following the repetition compulsion the participants want to push the conductor into a position which corresponds to the traumatic childhood scenario. One feels pressurized by this force and it is hardly possible to disentangle oneself from it. It so happened, for instance, that the women in Group 1 often seduced me and made me their ally in their fight against the men. My counter-transference consisted in that I sensed their desire to seduce me and I also registered in myself the inclination to let myself be seduced. Up to a certain point I even entered the scene they unconsciously set up. Through the collusion with the conductor the family configuration became directly apparent. This is the configuration that several members in most groups have experienced as traumatic in their childhood. The conductor should be able to recognize − if not in the same session, then at least before the next session starts − what the group 'did to' him. He should translate this discovery into an interpretation. By interpreting he dissolves the scenario and helps the participants involved to gain insight.

This way of using counter-transference is easiest when participants, as in Group 1, suffer from transference neurosis. There was a phase in which the men in Group 1 launched a massive attack against the women, provoking corresponding reactions among the latter. The men tried to draw me into their attack against the women. I felt in my counter-transference partly like a man who rapes, partly like a woman who is raped. Thereupon, I gave the following interpretation which the group was able to accept: 'The men here are raping the women. The mood is like when a penis wants to force its way into a vagina.' The prerequisite for this interpretation was that I had allowed myself to follow with my feelings what the participants wanted to 'do to' me. I did not go, however, as far as to play their game, namely to attack the women. In such a situation the conductor has to perform the following tasks: first he has to perceive the onset of the game. Then he has to examine it in the light of his theoretical frame of reference and the state of the group process. Finally he translates his conclusions into an interpretation. In a later phase of the group process, in which Mr Gage violently attacked me, I had the feeling of being in a fight between father and mother. At the same time Mrs Faulkner recalled that her father had often been attacked by her mother. The group was experiencing Mr Gage and myself as fighting parents. I gave this interpretation, which must have been the right one, as the great tension in the group disappeared soon afterwards.[3]

The use of counter-transference is more difficult in a narcissistic group like Group 2. As has been mentioned, Heinz Kohut's[4] practical and theoretical considerations apply very well to such groups. Thus, the counter-transference in a narcissistic group is a reaction to idealizing transferences. The latter can mobilize unintegrated grandiose ideas in the conductor which he finds unpleasant. As a result he rejects them and in so doing he disappoints the group and their idealized expectations.

The situation is most difficult for the analyst when he has to face a group whose members are out to 'do to' him what their parents did to them. Such was Group 3. Here the participants, and among them especially Marian, tried again and again to devalue the conductor, by disregarding him and by discrediting his interpretations as 'banal'. In his counter-transference the conductor does react to this contempt and devaluation and he has to have sufficient self-confidence not to let himself be affected by it all. This is not always easy. At times it was hard to bear the devaluation of my person by Marian who considered me totally incapable of helping the group in any way. It is not that one should not feel this devaluation. What matters in such a group is that one should be able to understand the feeling of devaluation in the counter-transference. This feeling of being devalued is a signal indicating that a deeply ambivalent mother-child relationship — with precise characteristics arising from the participants' original experience — has established itself in the relationship between the group and the conductor. If participants had felt in childhood unwanted and unloved, not valued, not respected and shoved off on to foster parents, then the conductor cannot expect anything else than that all that rejection will be turned against him. All those feelings the participants experienced in their childhood are now turned against the conductor in an 'identification with the aggressor'.[5] The participants do to him now what once was done to them. One can also say that the children, whom the participants once were, take revenge on the parents by hitting the conductor in their place. At the same time the group members — who are in the sub-layer IIc of our three-layers-model — experience the conductor as the mother who devalued and neglected them. If individual participants manage to free themselves from such a conductor — as happened in Group 3 — it is quite possible that this separation will bring progress for them. At least they manage to depart from the compulsive pattern that maintains them enmeshed with him in a sort of 'clinch', as they had been as children with their real mothers. They break out from the morbid repetition compulsion and, thus, liberate themselves from it.

5 The conductor's own transference to the group

There are not only transferences of the participants to the conductor and to his counter-transferences, but also transferences from the conductor's own childhood to the group. He will generally deny these transferences because they represent a capital error for a psychoanalyst. Nevertheless, such transferences do exist as Dieter Beckmann[6] convincingly proved through his experimental investigations with analysts. His results are ignored by many analysts, although the older generation of analysts were well aware of the existence of the analyst's transferences to his patients. Concerning group therapy, Walter Schindler openly admits that a participant made him particularly angry in a group, and he reported the incident in a scientific journal as early as 1955.[7] He saw no capital crime in such an anger which can sometimes arise from a very simple commonplace cause. What matters is that the conductor manages to see that he is in danger of favouring the group in a one-sided way to the cost of the participant who makes him angry.

Looking back at my work with the three groups, it is quite possible that I was not always able to react adequately to the destructive attacks of Mr Gage in Group 1 or to those of Marian in Group 3. It is also possible that my feelings of anger about these attacks were not only counter-transference, that is to say not only reactions to the transference of these participants. My anger could have arisen from my own transference to these participants to which they in their turn reacted. When this is the case, the rest of the participants feel that something is going on that does not belong directly to the group. Provided that the conductor discovers his own part in it and takes back the transference, there is no reason why this occurrence should harm the group process. In this respect group therapy is decidedly at an advantage *vis-à-vis* individual therapy. If a primary transference by the conductor to an individual member occurs, the rest of the group notices it and calls the conductor's attention to his transference. In Group 1 my own transference to Mr Gage was relatively insignificant. In this respect I was helped by the fact that the group itself perceived Mr Gage's behaviour as totally inadequate. In contrast, in Group 3 my own part of transference to Marian was greater and the group noticed it very well. I picked up the group's correct perception and admitted openly that I did have angry feelings in relation to Marian. This discussion relieved the group and promoted the group process.

Apart from the danger of favouring one group member or rejecting another, there is also the danger that, unconsciously, the conductor might use a participant or the group-as-a-whole to compensate for his own unfulfilled needs. In fact, a group can be not only a heavy personal burden — like Group 3 — but it can also give one profound satisfaction. This was the case with Groups 1 and 2 in which the process was progressive throughout. In such cases the analyst has to watch out that he does not make unconscious use of the group to compensate himself for his own childhood deprivations. Bernardo Blay Neto[8] points to the fact that 'the group [is] an excellent audience, in front of which the therapist's narcissistic or other needs find a splendid opportunity to express themselves and to be gratified.' It is important for the conductor to be aware of these more or less unconscious needs so that he can keep them at bay. It is advisable to have completely honest discussions about this problem with colleagues practising group therapy, to maintain a continual exchange of ideas with them, and to get at least occasional supervision from an experienced group therapist. Mild transferences of the conductor to the members of his group in the sense that he is fond of them and finds them likeable are quite legitimate. Such feelings correspond to what Sigmund Freud called the 'mild' or 'tender' transference[9] of the patient on to the analyst. In general, the group process works better when such mutual fondness exists. The working alliance is stronger and also feelings of hatred and aversion are easier to tolerate. Sooner or later these negative feelings are bound to arise through transferences in the great variety of sub-layers. On the other hand, it can be extraordinarily instructive for both parties, when someone who first appeared unlikeable becomes increasingly likeable. This person can be a group member as seen by the conductor or it can be the conductor as seen by a group member. This change in perception occurs in the course of the group process after the distorting transferences have been worked through. The experience is enriching for both sides. Feelings of liking and disliking, as they generally occur whenever people mix with each other, are not transference distortions and cannot be checked by taking back the transference. When such feelings are excessively pronounced and out of proportion and, moreover, differ from the feelings of other people, then one is entitled to suspect transferences. In order to free himself from such transferences, the analyst submits to a long post-graduate training which includes his own analysis. Therefore, the participation in a group process in the patient's role should be a *sine qua non* prerequisite for the training of a group therapist. It is only through his own experience that he can learn how he affects groups and how he is likely to make unconscious use of them. If he has no chance to participate in a therapeutic group, then he can become a member of an experiential group. Visits to group dynamics laboratories can also help to provide substantial learning experiences. The participants of such laboratories tell one another what effect they have and in which way they use their defences. For the group therapist the equivalent of training analysis, to which the psychoanalyst who works in individual therapy submits, is this participation in a sufficiently long group process. Only after such a training will he be in a position to relativize himself and his own behaviour; to assess the situation in the group independently from his own transferences; to make himself the object of his own observations; to analyse continually the interaction in the field of transference and countertransference; and to make the pertinent interpretations. Finally, in advanced phases of the group process especially during the end phase — which I will discuss later — the conductor has the chance of recognizing and changing some of his own behavioural patterns which interfere with his work. He can do this with the help of the group that has become mature enough, having learned to see more and more during several years of analytic process.

Chapter 15

The relationship between individuals, the psychoanalyst and the group

1 The level of the working relationship

If group therapy is indicated for a patient who seeks the psychoanalyst's help, that possibility will be put to him. Provided that the patient is ready to follow up the suggestion, an individual 'contract' will be agreed between him and the analyst. This 'contract' means that they both commit themselves to co-operate with the aim of attaining the objectives of therapy (see Chapter 1). Because of the particular kind of treatment, this 'contract' needs to be confirmed in the group situation. It is only in the group that the individual is together with other patients, and that the previous dyadic relationship is transformed into a multiple relationship. As this change can be stressful and needs adjustment on the patient's part, it is advisable that the analyst prepares him for the new situation.

Sometimes it is a colleague of the group therapist who conducts the preliminary 'interview' and suggests psychoanalytic group therapy to the patient. In these cases the conductor starts by facing not individuals but the group-as-a-whole in its already established composition. The 'contract' then is made only between the group and the conductor. This is the procedure followed, for instance, by Leon Grinberg, Marie Langer and Emil Rodrigué.[1] They meet the patient when he already belongs to the group. They avoid meeting him earlier in order to prevent transference relationships developing outside the actual group therapeutic situation. They even avoid learning about the patients' personal histories in order to concentrate completely on the relationship between the group and the conductor.

In my opinion one only can adopt such a procedure in an institution. An analyst working in a private practice cannot afford to handle his patients in this way simply because they would desert him. The psychotherapist with an established private practice has no choice but to deal with the individuals who come to see him either sent to him by a colleague or on their own. A conductor who works under these conditions, is not in a position to confine himself to the group and the group process as the only focus of his attention. He will constantly keep in mind each individual and his problems.

2 The relationship between individuals, the psychoanalyst and the group when a participant is in distress

Sometimes it occurs that certain situations of acute distress require the attention of the conductor and the group. In such a case the group takes care of the individual and his particular problem. This help leads to a dyadic relationship developing between him and the rest of the group. This relationship is equivalent to the relationship of a mother to her child. It happened, for instance, in the initial phase of Group 3, the students' group. In the eighth session Marian had a problem with her boy-friend who was having an homosexual relationship at the same time and wanted to leave the town where they both lived. Marian had to decide whether to go with him or not. This was a vital question for her. It also involved the decision of whether to continue or to inter-rupt her group therapy. Of course, by presenting her individual prob-lem she, as the group's 'speaker', unconsciously also expressed something of the group's problem and of its relationship with the conductor. There was a concealed question whether the group should interrupt or continue the therapy. I felt, however, that in this case the individual problem brought in from outside, and caused by the participant's friend, had to be given priority. Therefore, I let the group deal with Marian's topical question. After its great initial activity, the group became depressed and resigned when it became clear that Marian's dilemma could not be solved so quickly. After I fed back this observa-tion, Bill and Evelyn, two of the relatively least disturbed participants, managed to lead the group back to a more co-operative mood. This renewed co-operation enabled Marian to present her conflict in a clearer form, thus bringing it nearer to a solution. In the next session I interpreted the way the group had dealt with this individual partici-pant and vice versa. The group process as such had not been held up by this individual interlude.

As mentioned earlier in another context, during the thirty-first session of the same group, Eric was in a state of panicky fear of becom-ing a father. This anxiety was connected with his complete inability to work or to undertake any activity. Naturally, in his role as a 'speaker' of the group he too signalled something from the group to the conductor. The problem of the group was that it felt reluctant to take over a father's functions towards his child, for which it was in no way ready. On the other hand, Eric's problem was so pressing that I did not shrink from mentioning various possibilities of practical help he could get. I did so after half an hour's unsuccessful attempt on the part of the group to find a solution for him. It is important for the conductor to be aware of how the group feels after such an intervention. In a case like the one just described, the group – in its vain efforts to help – might feel like a person who fails completely. In other words, the group becomes the bad, not-good-enough part, while the conductor is the good, helping object who takes care of the individuals. Both these transference directions correspond to the characteristic transference split in sublayer IIc of our three-layers-model. The same configuration in another group might have been experienced unconsciously as a triadic Oedipal conflict with the group seen as the mother and the conductor representing the father. In conclusion when dealing with the problems of individual participants in distress, it is important to keep an equally watchful eye on the relationship between him and the other members as well as between the latter and the conductor. The therapist's own feeling of counter-transference together with his theoretical considerations on the state of the group process help him to recognize and interpret these relationships accordingly. If it goes well, the correctness of the interpretation will be confirmed by the fact that new memories will emerge and the process keep on unfolding. If the interpretation is not correct, the group will reject or ignore it.

3 The relationship between individuals, the psychoanalyst and the group when early childhood sexuality is reactivated – the perspective of the psychosis-model

In order to illustrate such a network of relationships, I will take an episode from the 141st session of Group 1. Mr Morgan starts the session with a rather contrived attack against the women while trying to come across as being very energetic and aggressive. He declares that a firm erect penis is something quite impressive for him. Mrs Sheen and Mrs Faulkner react by rejecting his statement. The rest of the male participants reinforce Mr Morgan's attitude and together with him build up a battle line against the female participants. I comment on this struggle between the sexes which is so obvious that I have no doubt whatsoever that my interpretation stands on a firm and unbiased psychoanalytic ground. Nevertheless the women react as if I had sided with the men. Mrs Faulkner remarks that Mr Morgan behaves in a downright silly fashion. The battle alignment between the sexes was, however, unmistakably there already in the seating arrangement. The women were drawn up in a semi-circle facing the men. Moreover, Mr Morgan pulled his chair forward in the women's direction. The pictorial result was that he was projecting into the group's circle as if he were an erect penis in an open vagina. Once I pointed out this seating arrangement and its visible shape, the group was able to accept my former interpretation about the struggle between the sexes as well as to work through the problem of the man's penetration into the woman.

In a later phase of the group process the same seating arrangement was experienced differently. This time the women's group represented a big mouth or a vagina that greedily wants to swallow everything, such as for instance a breast or a penis. The group then evokes images like those described by Melanie Klein in her child analyses[2] or those which occur in the analyses of psychotic adults. Participants are perfectly able to comprehend and to accept such an interpretation especially if they are shown compelling visible indicators like the seating arrangement. In addition, for the participants to accept the interpretation it is necessary that its 'depth' should not be too far removed from the level of the participants' current experience.

Practice in the therapy of mentally ill patients helps the conductor to grasp such scenes in the group that would appear bewildering to the average layman. It was Wolfgang Widok[3] who, on the strength of his many years of experience with groups, drew my attention to this aspect of our work. A conductor who is also a psychiatrist, can understand a deeply regressed group far better than someone who is not familiar with psychiatric patients. When dealing with such a group he will feel in the same way as when he sits facing a schizophrenic patient. Participants unconsciously perceive themselves as parts of mother's or father's body and the group-as-a-whole behaves exactly like a psychotic patient. From this perspective we can talk of a 'psychosis-model' of the group. The group's primitive functions in such a mood become clear if we look at them in the light of Melanie Klein's internal-object theory. It was Pierre Turquet, a visiting expert in group therapy from London who, in his supervision seminars at Tübingen, showed us convincingly how this kind of understanding of group processes works. His untimely death in 1975 was a lamentable loss for our field. In states of deep regression the group's scenario is dominated by the world of internal images, good and bad, protective as well as destructive, and also by corresponding fears of being completely swallowed, eaten up, destroyed or pushed out. The participants' ego seems to be swamped by internal images and put out of action. The shadows of the past have come to life to populate an uncanny spirit-world. In phases of such deep regression the conductor represents the very ego of the group and it is only through his eyes that participants are able to see reality. Nevertheless, it is possible to exorcize the threatening spirits, to bring them to the level of consciousness and integrate them into the participants' ego. The prerequisites facilitating this positive move are sufficient experience on the part of the conductor, a good working alliance between him and the group and a positive, though not too strong, transference on both sides (see Chapter 14,5).

4 The relationship between individuals, the psychoanalyst, and the group when childhood narcissism is reactivated — the perspective of the narcissism-theory of the group

As explained earlier (Chapters 7.3 and 9.2), the conductor represents an idealized parent imago in groups composed of participants who suffer from narcissistic personality disorders. This idealizing transference was especially evident in the initial phase of Group 2. In view of traumas received in their early childhood, nearly all participants could be classified within the 'post-classical' neuroses.[4] The relationship between such a group and the conductor is characterized by the fact that parts of the participants' grandiose selves are projected on to the group. When this projection occurs, the group appears particularly great to them. The more immature the projected elements of the grandiose self are, the more easily will such a perception lead to disillusionments in the group.

This process can take place in therapy groups as well as in other groups. It occurs whenever a group ventures upon insoluble tasks because it believes itself able to solve them. This belief stems from the group feeling unrealistically strong due to the unconscious mobilization of ideas of grandiosity. I had the opportunity to observe these processes time and time again in supervision groups with students of education and social work.[5] The same happened with many students at the peak of the student movement in Germany in the late 1960s. Many of them embarked on work with groups of convicts, mentally handicapped children, drug-addicts, runaways and vagrants. In most cases these students found that the task was far more demanding than they had anticipated. Severe disillusionments of clinical proportions ensued with depressions, resignation and mutual destructiveness. Groups split into subgroups and eventually dissolved, the same process as in our Group 3. In my opinion Horst Eberhard Richter's book *The Group* with its far too promising subtitle 'Hope for a New Path to Liberate Oneself and Others' has substantially contributed — at least in Germany — to elevate the group to the role of a grandiose self. On the other hand, one also finds in it such realistic views as those expressed in the following passage. Here the author points out the difficulties middle-class people encounter when they try to establish self-help groups among the homeless:[6]

> One has to deal with mechanisms and forces, [for] which one . . .
> is emotionally not quite prepared . . . one has to cut down . . .
> initial hopes [and] . . . acknowledge for once that one has
> approached an infinitely difficult task in an amateurish way . . . Of
> course, one can repress this insight into one's limitations and by
> being caught up in a hectic frenzy of activity for years, one can do
> many things without ever admitting to oneself that one is really
> getting nowhere. If one were able to face the painful insight,
> then . . . the summing up . . . would run: We are disillusioned with
> ourselves, we anticipated the [task] to be far easier. . . . Moreover,
> we realize that we as a group are not yet able at all to master
> problems that are so difficult.

5 The relationship between individuals, the psychoanalyst, and the group when early childhood aggressiveness is reactivated — the perspective of the borderline-theory of the group

In my students' group, Marian disputed the conductor's authority and at the same time sought salvation in the group. A phase of resignation ensued after the disappointing and inescapable recognition that the ideals could not be attained. In this phase the group presented the chaotic picture (see Chapter 11.1) that according to Heinz Kohut[7] corresponds to the 'fragmented self' and the 'archaic forms of idealization'. The chaos worsened even further when after only five sessions, following the four weeks' summer holiday, I had to interrupt the process yet again for a further four weeks. In the first session after this interruption — the twenty-sixth in the group's life — there was a small core group which had maintained its cohesion. This group felt like a torso that has been robbed not only of its 'limbs' — the missing group members — but also of its head, namely the conductor. The absent participants returned in the next session, some of them arriving very late. Somehow the group did not come together to form a whole, but it remained split in subgroups competing with each other. At the same time participants' symptoms worsened. Relief was only felt when Lucy, who had been absent for eight weeks, reappeared quite unexpectedly. Now it was possible to express the aggressiveness that had been defended against vigorously during the previous period of deprivations. For instance, Bill was able to tell of his dream in which a cow with a knife in her head was led to be slaughtered. The associations, produced mostly under Marian's direction, brought out mutual destruction. In accordance with her political ideology, she equated this mutual destruction with class struggle. The class struggle was directed in the first place against the representative of the 'haves', namely the conductor. Marian underscored her verbal attacks with treading on the conductor's ashtray. In subsequent phases her transference was characterized by cold rejection. Once the conductor and the group had been devalued to this extent, the participants could not do anything else for the time being but look for help from objects outside the group. Only Ursel, the participant who had joined only recently, managed to bring the group to see clearly what it had done, by holding up a mirror to it. Thereupon the group recovered from its weeks' long, near deadly crisis. As already mentioned (see Chapter 11.3), during this period of recovery individual participants managed to achieve substantial progress in mastering their concrete life problems. The prerequisite was that the fragmented group, which was falling apart because of internal struggle, could regain the feeling of being held together. In Heinz Kohut's terminology the group's 'fragmented self' was replaced by a 'cohesive self'.

This change was manifest already in the next session, the forty-sixth, which started with a long silence. There was perplexity about destructive forces in the group as well as a sincere desire to make up for what had been destroyed. After Eric had summoned up the courage to express his feelings openly, silence set in once more. I interrupted it quietly with the observation that the group was regaining its trust.

Thereupon other participants too were able to talk about their fear of contact, of independence, of obligations and responsibility. These contributions were made in an atmosphere of mutual respect and attentive listening, and intervals of thoughtful silence. I interpreted the silence as an unspoken desire to be accepted and understood and as the sign of a new trust placed in me and in the others.

In such phases participants expect the conductor to put their feelings into words and thus to help them to understand what the group-as-a-whole feels. Anna Freud calls this very important process the verbalization of feelings.[8] If successful, it helps participants, theoretically speaking, to build up in themselves 'representatives' for those feelings and to integrate them into their ego structures. In other words, once the emotions experienced in the preceding situation are internalized, they become objectivized in the individuals' psyche. In other words, they become additional elements that build the personality and broaden the existing structure.

In this session there were also signs of the so-called mirror transference as described by Heinz Kohut.[9] We speak of mirror transference when participants see their feelings reflected in the conductor. Once the conductor verbalizes these feelings — and only then — the participants begin to acknowledge and accept them and in this way they liberate themselves. This is how split-off, destructive forces can be accepted in a less destructive form, followed by a noticeable stabilization of individual participants (see Chapter 7.3).

6 The relationship between individuals, the psychoanalyst, and the group and the participants' ability to be members of the group — the perspective of the family-model

When transference neuroses prevail, as in Group 1, the group experiences the areas on to which participants are unconsciously fixated. These are the psychic points at which group members did not manage to overcome painful early childhood experiences they suffered within their families. Each participant feels as a member of the original family group. I have already mentioned this 'family model' several times (see Chapters 7.3; 8 and 13.2). In the course of the group process dominant problems appeared — specific to each group — which, through transference splits, affected the relationships among participants. In Group 1 it was the conflicts between mother, father and child; in Group 2, it was problems of self-esteem participants had as

children in relation to their parents; in Group 3 the split-off object-
and self-parts that had not been integrated into the ego. Dieter Ohlmeier[10] explains very clearly these processes, which can occur at
different stages of development, on differing levels of maturity. He
assumes that in addition to the developmental line that moves towards
a well-defined ego-identity, there is another, special developmental
line of the ego which he calls 'group-ego-function'. This concept helps
us to understand how traumatic situations are re-experienced in the
here and now of the group, that is to say how the past reappears in the
present. The concept of 'group-ego-function' implies that the individual's trauma corresponds always to a family trauma. Given the appropriate emotional climate, it is painfully re-enacted in a regression 'in
the group's service',[11] as if it were the real trauma. In this way the
individuals' ego becomes linked with that of the group through the
'group-ego-functions'[12] which led it to relive the traumatic situation
in the family. In the traumatic scene, which is reproduced, each individual can work through — *a posteriori* — the traumas he suffered as a
member of his family.

Just as in individual analysis, this work is done directly at the ego
level and through the ego. It seems to me that this process should dis-
prove the doubts of those who believe that in groups the ego is
switched off as in hypnosis,[13] while the id is active in most events. As
in individual analysis the work at the ego-level stretches over a long
period. In Group 1 it lasted for over three-and-a-half years, from
November 1969 to the end of July 1973, with 200 sessions of 100
minutes each. This is a span of time not essentially shorter than the
one required for classical psychoanalytic processes. With psychoanalytic group therapy we can attain results comparable to those of
individual analysis, provided that each traumatic family situation is
overcome through patient, meticulous, constant 'remembering, repeating and working through'.[14] In this way participants who are
fixated to Oedipal situations — like those in Group 1 — are able to solve
such conflicts *a posteriori*. Also narcissistic injuries left over from
earlier slights — as in the case of the participants of Group 2 — can be
healed little by little. As time goes by and their co-operation progessively improves, the members of the group can learn to understand
these mortifications which are re-experienced in the current situation.
Then they can also try a kind of 'new beginning'[15] in which they
respect each other and avoid inflicting new injuries. Similarly, in Group
3 participants were able to recognize that the split-off, destructive
forces were part of their own personalities. The destructive forces

could assume more mature forms soon after they had been verbalized in communications by group members and the conductor. Even if the group itself fell victim to the stress of destructiveness, the destructive forces could be accepted and integrated in the participants' personalities.

Despite the many differences between the three groups, there was one common feature: in the course of the group processes each participant's crucial childhood relationships reappeared and were relived in his relationship with the conductor and with other group members.

Chapter 16
The end phase of the group process

1 Fundamental theoretical considerations

The termination of a psychoanalytic group therapy is as vexed a question as that of an individual analysis. Not long ago Friedrich Wilhelm Eickhoff[1] carried out special research into this problem. Among other aspects, he discusses in his study the exact criteria that help to assess whether the objectives of an analysis have been attained. There are several such criteria also for psychoanalytic group therapy. They should help to decide whether the therapeutic process, having attained its objectives, can be terminated. The main criteria are:

i.   The symptoms that prompted the patient to seek the psychoanalyst's help and to agree to group therapy, should have ceased. As we have seen, the symptoms disappear in the course of the group process, after the unconscious pathogenic conflicts, which caused the symptom, had been reactivated.
ii.   'The most favourable psychological conditions for ego-functioning'[2] should be established so that the ex-patient is able to feel independent and free to make his own decisions.
iii.   Having re-lived the 'forgotten' infantile conflicts and worked through them, the infantile amnesia should be lifted.
iv.   Having demolished projective distortions, the individual should be able to perceive reality as it is.
v.   Pathological resistances should be dissolved.[3]
vi.   The Oedipus complex in its positive and negative forms should be resolved to a reasonably large extent.
vii.   Finally, concerning sex identity, the 'rejection of femininity' should be replaced by a healthy feminine potency in the woman; and the passive-feminine position should be integrated into the active-masculine position in the man.

These seven criteria are valid for participants in a psychoanalytic therapy group to the extent to which they suffer from transference neuroses — as did most of the members of Group 1. In case of narcissistic personality disorders, as we have seen them in the participants of Group 2, the objectives are less ambitious. The major aim is to master the narcissistic problems through the idealizing transferences and the mobilization of the narcissistic self. This mastery is achieved when the person reaches the point at which he is able to recognize that he is not perfect, but has faults, weaknesses and imperfections, and yet he does not feel diminished in his self-esteem because of this insight, nor is he hurt when others call his attention to his imperfections. The treatment's objective for serious character disorders of the type of the 'borderline personality organization', as in Group 3, is even more modest. It consists in substituting a clear identity in the place of 'role diffusion'.[4] Reliable interpersonal relationships should replace the disturbed ones. Finally, the characteristic split between good and bad impulses should be overcome leading to a unity in which more or less good, and more or less bad parts of the personality come together in an integrated fashion.

When the group process draws near to its objective, then the end phase has begun. One can recognize it by the fact that individual participants start to broach the question of termination. Others sum up the group process as such, or return to muse upon problems which have already been settled. Past interpretations that have not been understood sufficiently, come up for discussion and misunderstandings are clarified. In this phase it is imperative for the analyst openly to admit the mistakes, blunders and slips of attention for which he may have been responsible in the past. Such admissions unfailingly lead to a relieving of the participants' anxieties.

The conductor too is unburdened in the end phase. By working through the transference neuroses, gradually he becomes a real, significant object for the participants. In other words the transference pressure on him diminishes. What takes place is the 'resolution'[5] of the transference and with it a 'movement towards freedom'.[6] This process 'has as its precondition the lifting of the counter-transference [on the part of the therapist]'.[7] In order to take back the counter-transference, the conductor has to distance himself progressively from the group and the individual participants. This task can only be achieved by experiencing and working through the pain of separation and a period of mourning. It also requires that the analyst 'is able to be alone, without feeling lonely'.[8] This capacity of being alone is even more important for group conductors than for the psychoanalyst who works with individual patients only. As mentioned earlier (see Chapter 14.5), since a great part of the group process centres round the conductor, it is unavoidable that he gets a certain measure of narcissistic gratification out of it. He has to renounce this gratification gradually during the end phase. If the conductor fails to do so, group members remain attached to him too long like children whose parents do not want to give them up. If the conductor, however, makes this 'advance contribution',[9] then he will be in a better position to understand the group's reactions to the impending termination of the analysis. Among these reactions there is nearly always disappointment because of the conductor's alleged cold-heartedness. In the participants' perception he drops them 'like hot potatoes' and once more their symptoms might flare up as well. Nevertheless, group members will be able to detach themselves eventually as the concealed reproaches regarding the therapist's withdrawal are worked through.

The best solution is when both parties, the group as well as the therapist, together reach the mutual understanding that it is time to terminate the work.[10] According to Hal T. Turn,[11] this point is reached when the patient wishes to be again his own master, separated from the analyst. If this separation is difficult in individual analysis, it is even more so in group analysis. In the group several persons are involved, some of whom are more advanced in the process than others. Should the advanced members 'get off' earlier or should they continue participating out of solidarity with the rest? If they stay on, then the question arises of whether they disturb the group process by rousing guilt feelings in the others or by standing in their way. These problems have to be worked through together in the here and now of the group situation.

In my experience one can keep a group together as a whole up to the termination of the process. The condition is that individual participants' impulses to detach themselves are seen and worked through in relation to the group process. Behind wishes to terminate there are often concealed remains of passive desires, against which participants defend themselves. It can be residual desires for dependence, and anxieties *vis-à-vis* independence and responsibility. If these desires are interpreted in relation to the group as the reference point, then the interest of those participants who feel that they are ahead of the others will be sustained.

According to Ernst A. Ticho,[12] one has to distinguish two consecutive steps in the end phase. First, a mutual understanding between the patient and the therapist – in our case, between the group and the conductor – has to be reached and, second, the termination date has to be fixed. From the group's reaction to the impending end, the conductor can ascertain how far the group has progressed – or how far it has still to go to attain the above-mentioned objectives. If, for instance, there is very intense disillusionment because of the relapse into the old symptoms, then the process should not yet be terminated. If, on the other hand, this disillusionment is not excessive and the group is able to bring up for discussion any temporary worsening of symptoms, then the time for termination has come.

2 The end phase of Group 2

As an example for the end phase of a group process, let us see what happened in Group 2. Already months before the end, some participants began to think of the group's termination. The 145th session illustrates very well their reactions as the end drew closer. Albert starts with a question directed at the group: 'On which date exactly will we finish?' If he may say something about it, he personally would like to carry on up to the summer holidays. While Mary agrees, Gisela declares that she cannot tune in with the idea of an end. After that Ralph states that he is not satisfied at all with the results obtained so far and would like to progress further. After some silence Albert takes up again the question he asked at the beginning of the session. He finds himself thinking more of his wife and family. One day the group has to stop. At this point I say that I had considered the end of June as the termination date for the group. Silence sets in. Then George, who has not yet spoken, starts to talk about his dying boss. A sad mood spreads in the group. A contribution by William ensues, apparently coming from a totally different direction. Making a reference to previous sessions, he tells the group that he recently visited a former teacher of his and he is quite happy about the talk they had. He managed to express the things that distressed him at school and the teacher too could see some of his points. After a pause he adds that he had a dream, he dreamed of everything gold, pure gold. Having expressed already his dissatisfaction with some participants' wish to terminate, Ralph starts again. He has dreams of persecution and is full of hatred towards the church. He would never take his parents to live with him even if they were very sick. It would be just too loathsome.

During the further course of the session other participants too talked about their relationship with their parents. Two sub-groups emerged from this discussion. One took an independent and at the same time conciliatory position *vis-à-vis* their parents. The other sub-group led by Ralph held out in its position of total disavowal. I first linked the participants' relationship to their parents with the here and now of the group situation. Then I gave the following transference interpretation: Evidently some of the members are quite satisfied with the success we achieved, wish to become independent and are ready to part from me in a spirit of reconciliation. Others, on the contrary, feel that they are left in the lurch. They find I am heartless when I leave them to their own devices. They react with rage and hatred to the prospect of being left alone. They do not dare to express this rage directly against me, but they can talk about it by displacing it to their parents or the church. This hatred, especially in the case of Ralph, rouses the fear of being punished or persecuted for it. We have still time up to the end of the group to work on this hatred and anxiety.

In fact, thereafter and throughout the last months the group dealt intensively with the question of separation. Due to deaths in the families of two group members, this problem became even more acute. When these two members talked about what happened, the rest of the participants identified with them and experienced together with them, the feeling of being left alone. Some of them wept while expressing these feelings. The group as a whole effectively managed to work through a period of mourning.

In the 148th session there were once more expressions of bad temper. Mary reproached the group because of her renewed vomiting. Ralph was furious with me for letting him down. Gisela declared that in her mind she had already written off the group and is no longer really 'there'. The general mood and these statements were interpreted as follows: Now one can see clearly the disappointment with me because I agreed to the termination. There is equal disappointment with those members who picked up the theme of termination. Finally, there is probably disappointment with oneself as well because with the separation one is going to lose something and because one is perhaps also anxious about independence. The group reacts to all this, partly with depression, partly with aggression and partly with indifference.

At the start of the next session there is aggressive tension which does not seem to lessen. Then someone says laughingly: 'It is like the wolf and the seven kids. We are afraid to be eaten if we leave here.' The desire for an imperishable possession becomes clear when Ralph says: 'I still miss something I have not yet received.' In subsequent sessions the group is able to laugh about its anxieties and see them just as a relapse into problems vanquished long ago. Mary's vomiting subsided for good after we understood how often she had felt let down by the group. This was exactly the same feeling she had earlier in life in relation to her drunkard father and unstable mother. Once more the group went through a spell of dissatisfaction and reproaches. Led by Ralph, several participants kept on insisting that they should receive something concrete from me. This wish was answered in the 155th session when, as mentioned earlier, the vicar brought bread and distributed it. The symbolic meaning of this act was clear: 'After all, we ourselves possess all that we want to have from the conductor.' As in the Lord's Supper the participants received something they could digest and transform into a piece of themselves. In this way they made a decisive step forward towards independence.

In a later session, the 159th, a fight breaks out between William and Albert. The former reproaches Albert for leaving the sessions far too quickly while lighting a cigarette, so that it looks as if he did not need the group any more. Then Mary who is now five months pregnant says: 'Yesterday I really enjoyed my food. I retained it and did not need to spit it out.' In this very moment Gisela enters the room about ten minutes late, dressed in black. She says that her father died of cancer. . . . She talks about how she looked after him in the hospital, but also what a disillusionment he had been earlier in her life, when he got drunk and how he kept her at home and, if she managed to go out at all, how he subjected her to questioning afterwards. He was jealous even when her mother chatted with her. Gisela was left with no other choice but to run away from home. After that she sinks into silence. Someone asks her whether she is sad. She replies: 'Yes'. Ralph says he simply cannot understand that. The wish uppermost in his mind is for his father to die as soon as possible. Gisela reacts by telling him the following. 'And yet, you know, it is sad when one's father dies. Afterwards you are so alone, even if he has done many things wrong. I have thought of it a lot since then and now I can understand him better in many respects. He himself had lost his father when he was a small child. That is why he was clinging so hard to mother.' William's reaction to this is that he is unable to understand why his mother married a weak man. Mary tells the group that her father and her mother married only when she was already on the way. She puts, however, the conciliatory question to the group: What else could her parents have done at the time? Some group members' dissatisfaction with their fathers was obvious and easy to interpret. As in the past the fathers were not on the spot when one needed them. In the group it has often been the same when one did not receive just what one needed. After this interpretation William says that he feels like crying. Albert talks about the guilt one has to feel when one is as hard towards a father as Ralph. Thereupon Ralph turns to me and says that I probably consider him a hopeless case. The women on the other hand stress that they received quite a lot from the group. Even Gisela who some weeks before had stated that the group did not mean much to her, and she was no longer 'there' at all, now says that she feels understood. She puts down my name in her address book. I sum it up: Despite the faults they discovered in me and in the others, several members are able to make something from the group and also to conserve it. This gain makes it easy for them to separate. Others, however, still have difficulties because they experience my behaviour as that of their fathers. As Ralph's relationship to his father is particularly difficult, I can well understand why he still has great difficulties in his relationship with me. Some participants had already told him that these difficulties might depend on guilt feelings or irreconcilable hatred because he did not receive what he is longing for so much. Perhaps he could find in himself the very things he is looking for. This was the end of the last session.

3 The end phase of Group 1

As I have outlined already the slow death of Group 3 (in Chapter 11), it only remains to present the end phase of Group 1. The members of this group had become increasingly independent: Mr Pittman felt more secure in his profession; Mr Morgan passed his exam; Mr Gage left the group in order to start individual therapy. Soon after that he gave up his profession and started a new career at the university. Only Mr Hardwick felt little improvement. He himself attributed his lack of progress to his difficulties in participating in the group process. Mrs Faulkner became very active professionally and through satisfaction in her work she managed to compensate for the lack of happiness in the relationship with her partner. Mrs Sheen separated from her husband. She found a far more satisfactory — though not entirely easygoing — relationship with another man who responded to her feelings. Mrs Sinfield moved to another town and to all appearances the relationship with her husband had improved.

The end phase of this group was heralded by Mrs Murphy telling the group that she had given notice at her work in order to go abroad. She would probably leave in about three months. Mr Pittman, the quiet man who earlier represented the group's conscience and now its critical ego-functions, pondered: 'Yes, that is what I thought too. It could work.' Mrs Faulkner and Mr Morgan behave at first in an ambivalent manner. Mr Hardwick, who still stammers, expresses his great worry about his child who also stammers. Mrs Sheen bursts into tears, once more accusing her husband for wanting to buy a car and for not seeing her needs.

This was a whole gamut of reactions to the first mention of the possible end of the group. The differences tallied with the various stages of development the group members had reached. The 192nd session gives a good picture of this diversity. The session is opened by Mr Morgan who tells the group how he is now in search of a woman and how he once went out with Mrs Faulkner and they had a good meal. Other group members talk about other equally gratifying occurrences. Finally, Mrs Murphy blurts out after having grown increasingly restless while listening: 'Stop it! All the talk here is irrelevant.' She had just come from a staff association council meeting, an election meeting. There it was clear that they were all afraid of management, the whole executive council of the staff association failed to turn up, leaving everyone else in the lurch. This fact hit her very much. Only the firm's boss put in an appearance. Mr Pittman comments: 'The one from the wrong side.' Mrs Sheen retorts: 'It is the stupidity of the people. They only want to eat and drink and do not see what happens around them.' After some minutes silence Mrs Murphy heaves a sigh and says: 'It would be better to run a soft drink booth. One would have no worries and plenty of time.' The group remains silent. I interpret: The members are searching for a substitute for the group and find the wrong people. This discovery is bitter because each participant is very much alone outside the group. Mrs Murphy: 'Yes, one is left alone in the struggle for more clarity and more influence.' Mrs Sheen: 'But one also wants to live and needs some compensation for all the effort.' Mrs Murphy, raising her voice: 'No. One has to shout, shout, shout!'. Silence follows which I interrupt with the question of how the group experiences me and what are its views as to what kind of things I would support. Mrs Sheen, the factory worker, replies: 'One can see that you are not a capitalist. You do sympathize.' Mr Pittman says: 'In my small firm I can defend myself. I could not do it if it were bigger.' Mrs Murphy: 'If we now had another four years before us, that would be nice. Everything requires such a frightful amount of time.' A depressed silence ensues interrupted by the journalist, Mrs Faulkner: 'All this is a burden for me. I've had enough of it. Now I want to live.' Thereupon Mr Hardwick: 'I am selfish and afraid of confrontations. I am only concerned with myself. I need not wonder why I have not made more substantial progress.' Mrs Faulkner again: 'I did progress because now I don't allow myself to be tortured any longer.' And finally Mrs Murphy says: 'I will have another go at the staff association, while I still have the group's support behind me.'

In the following session an agreement is reached that the group as a whole would stop working when Mrs Murphy leaves to go abroad. Mrs Faulkner incites the group to a kind of final spurt. She is convinced that one can solve and overcome the remaining difficulties and problems if everyone makes a special effort from now up to the very end. It is apparent that Mrs Sheen too is very committed. She is determined not to miss any sessions although her health insurance offered her a free holiday in a health resort which she would not like to forfeit either. She finds the solution by choosing a nearby resort. Inspired by the group's renewed commitment, I offer to meet twice a week for the final spurt instead of for the weekly sessions we have had up to now. The group immediately jumped at the offer. During the three months that followed no one missed a session. The intensity of the sessions was extraordinary. Resistances melted away one after the other. Participants were able to evoke past experiences which they had been shoving aside for years. While in the initial phase it had felt small and inferior, the group now felt great and superior to me. The participants no longer reported everything about themselves. They gave each other interpretations while I became increasingly dispensable. The distance between conductor and group members was decreasing continually. For instance the reports for the health insurance company were often discussed in the group. Whatever had to be done for the insurance, participants did it by themselves. Earlier in the group process (see Chapter 6.3) they were particularly helpless in this respect. Separated from her husband, Mrs Sheen found peace during her stay in the health resort. In a new relationship she also managed to experience orgasm which before she did not think would ever be possible. The group was now able to talk about sex far more openly than before. Even such aspects came up for discussion which previously had been dismissed as perversions. Some of the women expressed unequivocally their desire for oral sex and the desire to fondle the penis. At first the men reacted anxiously, but then they managed to say that they too saw new possibilities for their sex life which they had not dared to try out up to now.

Meanwhile the group worked through heavy mourning in view of the impending separation. For each member the group's anticipated death meant the loss of the conductor as well as parting from the other participants with whom he had become familiar. As a sort of final settlement of accounts the group reproached me in one of the sessions for having been cool and rejecting at the beginning. In that session the group managed to draw into the process the stammerer who up to then remained mostly outside the process. For the first time he was able to state that during the whole time he had been in the group he felt equally neglected by me as he had been by his father. Because of the fear of being rejected he never dared to push himself forward in the group. At the same time, recurrent fits of spasmodic coughing gave evidence of how his resistance began to weaken. In the last session which was the 205th, once more one was reminded of the old conflict between the sexes characteristic of this group. This time the conflict reappeared in the midst of a conciliatory mood.[13] The feelings towards me were a mixture of reproaches and gratitude: I was reproached for actually terminating the group's work, but the group was also grateful for what had been achieved. There was mourning and grief because of the group's death. It is only understandable that the conductor should take part in this mourning for the group which has been essentially his creation. It is the analyst who as its 'creator'[14] once upon a time had called it into being by selecting the group members and by making the contract with them in the first session. The hour of farewell had come. After nearly four years of shared work, one was going to separate in order to go alone each on his way.

I did not find it easy myself to say good-bye to the groups. The joy derived from the success we have attained, however, outweighed by far the pain of separation. These feelings are not unlike those of the parents when they set free into independence the children who have grown up.

Chapter 17
After group therapy has ended

1 Advantages of a concentrated individual therapy subsequent to group therapy

A group offers such a variety of experiences and facilitates such a host of transference relationships that only a fraction of it all can possibly be worked through individually in the course of the tightly packed time of the group process itself. A good way to make up for what one might have missed out, is to have a brief individual therapy immediately following the group therapy. This therapy should be a focal therapy[1] concentrating exclusively on the unsolved problems left over from the group process. Such a therapy helps the individual to recognize in its full personal significance whatever problem has been stirred up in the course of the group process and work it through in retrospect and in relation to his own life history. Subsequent to the termination of Group 3, two participants had individual therapy with me for a year and they appeared to profit from it very much. After termination Ralph from Group 2 also came to see me for a series of ten individual sessions. We discussed his group experiences exclusively in relation to his person. He had written me a letter: 'You too, as a therapist, you let me down today just as my father did. As once at school, so today I have to stand my ground alone in the fight with colleagues. Unfortunately you cannot help me to beat the oppressors black and blue.' Since that time he had become more independent, well able to handle his differences with colleagues. Now he could communicate and exchange views with his parents and, as he put it, he managed to 'exorcize his tormentors at last'.

In some cases of relationship problems with the partner, it is appropriate to have therapy as a couple after one of the two has had group therapy. Mr Morgan from Group 1 together with his wife sought such therapy. It helped them to tackle problems in their relationship openly and to find workable solutions.

2 Outcome of psychoanalytic group therapy

As several years have elapsed since these three groups finished their work, it is natural to raise the question of how much the individuals benefited from participating in the group process. To what extent has the group helped each of them to solve unconscious conflicts and, thus, not only to lose symptoms, but also to gain insight into himself and his relationships with others. Follow-up interviews would be an attractive proposition, but they are out of the question in psycho-analysis, the patient's objective being to free himself from the analyst, and rightly so. For this reason I know rather little about the further course of events in the lives of the members of the three groups. The little I learned in the intervening years, after the work in the three groups has ended, might convey, however, at least some idea about the possibilities and limits of psychoanalytic group therapy.

From the former Group 3 Evelyn sought consultation with me twice. She had a new partner and the relationship seemed to be far more mature than with her husband. She passed her education exams. I heard that Ursel had set herself free from her symbiotic relationship with her partner and was now studying.

From among the ex-members of Group 1 Mr Gage asked me to give him a reference to enter a course in a training college. He managed to ask this favour without resentment or bitterness. Meanwhile he had found a girl-friend with whom he had a good mutual understanding. When a child guidance clinic requested information from my records on Mrs Sinfield, I learned that she had consulted the clinic because of difficulties with her children. Her problems with her partner were not completely solved either. About a year after the group was ter-minated, Mrs Sheen came to see me in my consulting room at short notice. She was shattered because her new boy-friend let her down, having been unable to free himself from a pathological attachment. She had a healthy cry and collected herself ready to face the new situation. Mrs Murphy wrote me a letter from abroad. She had to decide now whether to stay on or return home. 'It is not easy to find an answer to this question. Yet as soon as I am able to make this decision, everything else will fall into place.'

These glimpses into ex-participants' lives show that a psychoanaly-sis – whether it is individual or group analysis – does not spare problems for the patient. It can only create a better basis to enable the patient to solve those problems on his own. Just when the German edition of this book was going into print I received a letter from Mr Morgan. He wrote about a promotion in his job and added: 'With this promotion I stepped over the threshold of average achievement. . . . In this respect the group helped. . . . My belated thanks.'

About half a year after the termination of the work in Group 2, Mary paid me a visit. She was overjoyed with her three-month-old child whom she brought with her to show to me. She also wanted to express her thanks for the success of her group therapy. Albert wrote to me: 'During the last weeks many things have become clear to me. One insight startled me especially because it was so simple. In retrospect I have to ask myself why I could not see it before. As you might remember I spoke in the group about my inability in dreams to rush from a height into the depth. Now I suddenly recalled the accident with great clarity, how — sitting in the child's seat in front on father's bicycle — I stormed into the valley and, down at the bottom of the hill, where the opposite slope begins to rise, the mishap took place. Telling it like that it appears trivial. Yet for me this single realization, with all that it implies, makes the whole effort that we invested in the group worthwhile.'

3 A concluding remark

It is my hope that these basic aspects of psychoanalytic group therapy will offer the reader a glimpse into this interesting field. Despite the subjectivity of judgment and experience through which these aspects have been presented, I trust that a sufficiently clear picture has emerged showing what psychoanalytic group therapy is. Perhaps the group therapist himself can use some of the techniques described in his own practice. To conclude with a word of self-evaluation, I think I would have worked slightly differently — especially in Groups 2 and 3 — had I been familiar at the time with the latest literature on the theory of narcissism and early object relations. Nevertheless, even in that case I do not think that the various group processes would have taken a substantially different course. The dynamics of a group process is determined by the individual problems and the personality structure of its members rather than by the conductor's theoretical frame of reference.

Notes

Preface to the German edition

1 'Aspekte der Gruppentherapie', *Psyche*, vol. 24 (1970), pp. 721-38;
'Übertragung und Prozess in der psychoanalytischen Gruppentherapie', *Psyche*, vol. 25 (1971), pp. 856-73; 'Über Paarbildung in
der psychoanalytischen Gruppentherapie', *Gruppenpsychotherapie
und Gruppendynamik*, vol. 6 (1972), pp. 125-33; 'Methoden
psychoanalytischer Gruppenarbeit', parts I, II, *Zeitschrift für
Psychotherapie und medizinische Psychologie*, vol. 23 (1973), pp.
15-23, 51-4.

1 Indication for treatment and the contract

1 R.R. Greenson, *The Technique and Practice of Psycho-Analysis*,
vol. 1, International University Press, New York, 1967.
2 K. Frank, 'Indikationen zur psychoanalytischen Gruppentherapie',
Psyche, vol. 22 (1968), pp. 778-85.
3 S. Freud, *Freud's Psychoanalytic Procedure*, standard edn, vol. 7,
p. 250.
4 S.H. Foulkes and E.J. Anthony, *Group Psychotherapy*, London,
1957, p. 29; S.H. Foulkes, *Therapeutic Group Analysis*, Allen &
Unwin, London, 1965.

2 Understanding, observing, interpreting

1 H. Ezriel, 'A psychoanalytic approach to the treatment of patients
in groups', *British Journal of Medical Psychology*, vol. 23 (1950),
pp. 59-74.
2 H. Argelander, 'Die Analyse psychischer Prozesse in der Gruppe',
Psyche, vol. 17 (1963-4), p. 481.
3 S. Freud, *Beyond the Pleasure Principle*, standard edn, vol. 18, p.
19.
4 A. Lorenzer, *Sprachzerstörung und Rekonstruktion*, Frankfurt,
1970, pp. 104ff.

114

5   S. Freud, *Three Essays on the Theory of Sexuality*, standard edn, vol. 7, pp. 123-243.
6   E.H. Erikson, *Childhood and Society*, Norton, New York, 1950, pp. 228-48.
7   P. Kutter, *Aspekte der Gruppentherapie*, pp. 729-33.
8   Especially R.A. Spitz, *The First Year of Life*, International Universities Press, New York, 1965; M.S. Mahler, *On Human Symbiosis and the Vicissitudes of Individuation*, International Universities Press, New York, 1968.
9   D.B. Lynn, *The Father: His Role in Child Development*, Brooks-Cole, Montery, Calif., 1974.

3 Three theoretical models of psychoanalytic group therapy

1   A. Wolf and E.K. Schwartz, *Psycho-Analysis in Groups*, New York and London, 1962.
2   H. Argelander, 'Die Analyse psychischer Prozesse in der Gruppe', *Psyche*, vol. 17 (1963-4), pp. 481ff.
3   P. Watzlawick, J.H. Beavin and D.D. Jackson, *Pragmatics of Human Communication*, Norton, New York, 1967.
4   'According to the uncertainty principle (Heisenberg, 1927) accurate measurement of an observable quantity necessarily produces uncertainties in one's knowledge of the values of other observables', *McGraw-Hill Encyclopedia of Science and Technology*, McGraw-Hill, New York, 1977, vol. 11, p. 165.
5   Argelander, op. cit., p. 487.
6   Goethe, *Faust*, Part 1 (Faust's study), trans. Philip Wayne, Penguin, Harmondsworth, 1973, (1st edn 1949), p. 95.
7   S.H. Foulkes, *Group Analytic Psychotherapy: Method and Principles*, Gordon & Breach, London, 1975.

4 The first session

1   H. Argelander, 'Gruppenanalyse unter Anwendung des Strukturmodells', *Psyche*, vol. 22 (1968), pp. 913-33.
2   Personal data are completely changed so as to guarantee anonymity in all cases.
3   H. Argelander, 'Gruppenanalyse – Einzelanalyse. Ein Vergleich', *Psychiatrie der Gegenwart, Forschung und Praxis*, vol. 3, 2nd edn, Berlin, 1975, p. 611.
4   H. Ezriel, 'A psychoanalytic approach to the treatment of patients in groups', *British Journal of Medical Psychology*, vol. 23 (1950), pp. 59-74.

6   Resistance and defence in psychoanalytic group therapy

1   W. Loch, 'Der Analytiker als Gesetzgeber und Lehrer', *Psyche*, vol. 28 (1974), pp. 446ff.
2   P. Kutter, 'Über moderne Neurosenformen und ihre gesellschaftliche Bedingtheit', in *Die Beziehung zwischen Arzt und Patient*, ed. S. Goeppert, Munich, 1975, pp. 215-16.
3   M. Balint, *The Basic Fault: Therapeutic Aspects of Regression*, Tavistock, London, 1968.
4   S. Freud, *Beyond the Pleasure Principle*, standard edn, vol. 18, p. 55.
5   E. Bibring, The conception of the repetition compulsion, *Psychoanalytic Quarterly*, vol. 12 (1943), pp. 468-519.

7   Transference in psychoanalytic group therapy

1   P.C. Kuiper, 'Zur Metapsychologie von Übertragung und Gegenübertragung', *Psyche*, vol. 23 (1969), p. 106.
2   D. Ohlmeier, 'Gruppenanalytische Übertragungsformen', paper given at the Central European Psychoanalytic Society meeting, Bad Aussee, 24 March 1970.
3   R.A. Spitz, *The First Year of Life*, International Universities Press, New York, 1965.
4   D.W. Winnicott, *The Maturational Process and the Facilitating Environment*, Hogarth Press, London, 1965.
5   M.S. Mahler *et al.*, *The Psychological Birth of the Human Infant*, Hutchinson, London, 1975, pp. 52-122.
6   W.R. Bion, *Experiences in Groups and other Papers*, Tavistock, London, 1961.
7   Ibid.
8   P. Kutter, 'Übertragung und Prozess in der psychoanalytischen Gruppentherapie', *Psyche*, vol. 25 (1971), p. 866.
9   H. Kohut, *The Analysis of the Self*, International Universities Press, New York, 1971.

8   The struggle with authority

1   M.S. Mahler, 'A study of the separation-individuation process and its possible application to borderline phenomena in the psychoanalytic situation', *The Study of the Child*, vol. 26, pp. 403-24.
2   B.D. Lewin, 'Phobic Symptoms and Dream Interpretation', *Psychoanalytic Quarterly*, vol. 21 (1952), pp. 295-322.
3   W. Loch, 'Der Analytiker als Gesetzgeber und Lehrer', *Psyche*, vol. 28 (1974), pp. 431-60.
4   A. Green, 'The analyst, symbolisation and absence of the analytic setting', *International Journal of Psychoanalysis*, vol. 56 (1975),

pp. 1-22.

5 P. Federn, 'Zur Psychologie der Revolution: Die vaterlose Gesell-
schaft', in *Der Aufstieg*, nos 11-12, Leipzig-Vienna, 1919. A.
A. Mitscherlich, *Society without the Father: a Contribution to
Social Psychology*. Trans. from the German by E. Mosbacher,
Tavistock, London, 1969.

6 P. Kutter, 'Über moderne Neurosenformen und ihre gesellschaftliche Bedingtheit', in *Die Beziehung zwischen Arzt und
Patient*, Munich, 1975, pp. 215-26.

7 M. Klein and J. Riviere, *Love, Hate and Reparation*, Hogarth Press
and the Institute of Psychoanalysis, London, 1937.

8 L. Grinberg, M. Langer and E. Rodrigué, *Psychoanalytische Gruppentherapie: Praxis und theoretische Grundlagen*, ed. W.W. Kemper,

9 Stuttgart, 1960.
S. Freud, *Remembering, Repeating and Working-Through*, standard
edn, vol. 12, pp. 147-56.

9 The group process: each individual participates in shared events

1 S.H. Foulkes, *Group Analytic Psychotherapy: Method and Principles*, Gordon & Breach, London, 1975.

2 Ibid.

3 P. Kutter, 'Übertragung und Prozess in der psychoanalytischen
Gruppentherapie', *Psyche*, vol. 25 (1971), p. 865.

4 Ibid., p. 859ff.

5 Foulkes, op. cit.

6 A. Heigl-Evers and F. Heigl, 'Gruppentherapie: interaktionell-
tiefenpsychologisch fundiert (analytisch orientiert)- psychoana-
lytisch', *Gruppenpsychotherapie und Gruppendynamik*, vol. 7
(1973), pp. 132-57.

7 W. Loch, 'Über theoretische Voraussetzungen einer psychoanalytischen Kurztherapie', *Jahrbuch der Psychoanalyse*, vol. 4 (1967),
pp. 82-101.

8 The term 'diatrophic' was introduced by René A. Spitz (1956) in
his paper on countertransference (*Journal of American Psychoanalytical Association*, 4, pp. 256-65) and means the analyst's response
to the patient's need for help. In the same way that a parent
responds to the anaclitic situation of the child, the analyst's
healing intention is to 'maintain and support' the patient (M.
Gitelson, 'The Curative Factors in Psychoanalysis', *International
Journal of Psychoanalysis*, vol. 43 (1962), p. 198).

9 Kutter, op. cit., p. 871.

10 H. Kohut, *The Analysis of the Self*, International Universities Press,
New York, 1971.

11 H. Kohut, 'Thoughts on Narcissism and Narcissistic Rage', *The
Study of the Child*, vol. 27 (1972), pp. 360-400.

12 H. Argelander, 'Gruppenanalyse – Einzelanalyse. Ein Vergleich', in
Psychiatrie der Gegenwart: Forschung und Praxis, vol. 3, 2nd edn,

Berlin, 1975, p. 611.
13 J. Willi, *Die Zweierbeziehung*, Rowohlt, Reinbek, 1975.
14 A. Green, 'The analyst, symbolisation and absence of the analytic setting', *International Journal of Psychoanalysis*, vol. 6 (1975).
15 S. Freud, *Papers on Technique, on Beginning Treatment*, standard edn, vol. 12, pp. 123-44.
16 S. Freud, *Remembering, Repeating and Working-Through*, standard edn, vol. 12, pp. 147-56. Cf. also A. Uchtenhagen, 'Erinnern, Wiederholen, Durcharbeiten in der Gruppenpsychotherapie', *Gruppenpsychotherapie und Gruppendynamik*, vol. 4 (1970), pp. 124-32.
17 S. Freud, *Analysis, Terminable and Interminable*, standard edn, vol. 23, pp. 216-52.

10 Early mother-child relationship in the group

1 L. Grinberg, M. Langer and E. Rodrigué, *Psychoanalytische Gruppentherapie. Praxis und theoretische Grundlagen*, ed. W.W. Kemper, Stuttgart, 1960.
2 O.F. Kernberg, 'Borderline Personality Organization', *Journal of the American Psychoanalytic Association*, vol. 15 (1967), pp. 641-85.
3 O.F. Kernberg, 'Psychoanalytic Object-relations Theory, Group Processes and Administration', *Annual of Psychoanalysis*, vol. 1 (1973), pp. 363-88, esp. 367ff.
4 P. Turquet, 'Threats to Identity in the Large Group', in L. Kreeger (ed.), *The Large Group: Dynamics and Therapy*, Constable, London, 1975, pp. 87-144.
5 H. Roskamp, 'Über Identitätskonflikte bei im Zweiten Weltkrieg geborenen Studenten', *Psyche*, vol. 23 (1969), pp. 754-61.
6 Kernberg, op. cit. (1967).

11 Self-destruction of a group or the result of constructive separations?

1 O.F. Kernberg, 'Borderline Personality Organization', *Journal of the American Psychoanalytic Association*, vol. 15 (1967), pp. 641-85.
2 M. Klein, *Contributions to Psycho-Analysis, 1921-1945*, Hogarth Press, London, 1948.
3 O.F. Kernberg, 'Prognostic considerations regarding borderline personality organization, *Journal of the American Psychoanalytic Association*, vol. 19 (1971), pp. 593, 635; also 'The treatment of patients with borderline personality organization', *International Journal of Psychoanalysis*, vol. 49 (1968), pp. 600-19; and *Borderline Conditions and Pathological Narcissism*, Jason Aronson, New York, 1975.

4   Goethe, *Faust,* Part 1 (Faust's study), trans. P. Wayne, Penguin, Harmondsworth, 1973 (1st edn 1949), p. 75.

12 Sexuality and the Oedipus complex in the group

1   P. Kutter, 'Übertragung und Prozess in der psychoanalytischen Gruppentherapie', *Psyche,* vol. 25 (1971), pp. 856-73, esp. 867-71.

13 Aggressiveness in the group

1   W. Schindler, 'Family Pattern in Group Formation and Therapy', *International Journal of Group Psychotherapy,* vol. 1 (1951), pp. 100-5.
2   D.W. Winnicott, *The Maturational Process and the Facilitating Environment,* Hogarth Press, London, 1965.

14 The conductor's function

1   H. Kohut, *The Analysis of the Self,* International Universities Press, New York, 1971.
2   A. Heigl-Evers and F. Heigl, 'Rolle und Interpretationsstil des Gruppenpsychotherapeuten', *Gruppenpsychotherapie und Gruppendynamik,* vol. 5 (1972), pp. 152-71, esp. 156ff.
3   P. Kutter, 'Methoden psychoanalytischer Gruppenarbeit, Part I: Methoden psychoanalytischer Gruppentherapie', *Zeitschrift für Psychotherapie und medizinische Psychologie,* vol. 23 (1973), pp. 20ff.
4   Kohut, op. cit.
5   A. Freud, *The Ego and the Mechanisms of Defence,* Hogarth Press, London, 1937.
6   D. Beckmann, *Der Analytiker und sein Patient,* Vienna, 1974, pp. 43-8.
7   W. Schindler, 'Gegenübertragung in der "Family Pattern" – Gruppenpsychotherapie', *Zeitschrift für Psychosomatische Medizin,* vol. 1 (1955), pp. 130-4, esp. p. 131.
8   B.B. Neto, 'Zur Gegenübertragung in der Gruppentherapie', *Zeitschrift für Psychosomatische Medizin,* vol. 12 (1966), pp. 138-43, esp. 139.
9   S. Freud, *The Dynamics of Transference,* standard edn, vol. 12, p. 101; *Remembering, Repeating and Working-Through,* standard edn, vol. 12, p. 151.

15 The relationship between individuals, the psychoanalyst and the group

1 L. Grinberg, M. Langer and E. Rodrigué, *Psychoanalytische Gruppentherapie: Praxis und theoretische Grundlagen*, ed. W.W. Kemper, Stuttgart, 1960.
2 M. Klein, *Narrative of a Child Analysis*, Hogarth Press, London, 1961.
3 Personal communication, 1975.
4 P. Kutter, 'Moderne Neurosenformen und ihre gesellschaftliche Bedingtheit', in *Die Beziehung zwischen Arzt und Patient*, Munich, 1975, pp. 215-26.
5 P. Kutter, *Sozialarbeit und Psychoanalyse*, Göttingen, 1974.
6 H.E. Richter, *Die Gruppe*, Rowohlt, Reinbek, 1972, p. 292.
7 H. Kohut, *The Analysis of the Self*, International Universities Press, New York, 1971.
8 A. Freud, *Normality and Pathology in Childhood*, International Universities Press, New York, 1965.
9 Kohut, op. cit.
10 D. Ohlmeier, 'Gruppenpsychotherapie und psychoanalytische Theorie', in *Gruppentherapie und soziale Umwelt*, Bern, 1975, pp. 548-57, esp. 552.
11 Ibid.
12 Ibid.
13 H. Kohut, personal letter, 1 January 1972.
14 S. Freud, *Remembering, Repeating and Working-Through*, standard edn, vol. 12, pp. 147-56.
15 M. Balint, *Primary Love and Psychoanalytic Technique*, Tavistock, London, 1963.

16 The end phase of the group process

1 F.W. Eickhoff, 'Probleme der Beendigung psychoanalytischer Behandlungen', in *Die Beziehung zwischen Arzt und Patient*, ed. S. Goeppert, Munich, 1975, pp. 92-108.
2 S. Freud, *Analysis, Terminable and Interminable*, standard edn, vol. 23, p. 250.
3 Eickhoff, op. cit., p. 101.
4 E.H. Erikson, *Childhood and Society*, Norton, New York, 1950.
5 W. Loch, *Voraussetzungen, Mechanismen und Grenzen des psychoanalytischen Prozesses*, Bern, 1965, p. 61.
6 Ibid., p. 63.
7 Ibid., p. 61.
8 Ibid., p. 44.
9 Ibid., p. 61.
10 'Problems of Termination in the Analysis of Adults', reported by S.K. Firestein, *Journal of the American Psychoanalytic Association*, vol. 17 (1969), p. 235.
11 H.T. Turn, 'Adolescent Transference', *Journal of the American*

Psychoanalytic Association, vol. 18 (1970), pp. 342-57, esp. 348.
12 E.A. Ticho, 'Probleme des Abschlusses der psychoanalytischen Psychotherapie', *Psyche*, vol. 25 (1971), pp. 44-56, esp. 53.
13 H. Stierlin, *Conflict and Reconciliation*, New York, 1969.
14 Eickhoff, op. cit., p. 105.

17 After group therapy has ended

1 D. Malan, *A Study of Brief Psychotherapy*, Tavistock, London, 1963; M. Balint, P.H. Ornstein and E. Balint, *Focal Psychotherapy: An Example of Applied Psychoanalysis*, Tavistock, London, 1972.

Index